Praise for *Building Spiritual Habits in the Home*

This book is not just refreshingly practical, it's ridiculously practical. Whenever I talk about *Habits of the Household*, I get asked: "But how do I start?" This book is going to be my new answer.

JUSTIN WHITMEL EARLEY, business lawyer, speaker, and author of *Habits of the Household*

The GoodKind team is a friend to those seeking how to best enter into discipleship within their family. What Chris and Clayton have written here is clear and practical, filled with expert advice. But it's also warm, accessible, relatable. They make your next steps clear—not for the sake of checking a box, but to cultivate intentional practices that help families grow closer to God and to each other. This truly is an incredible resource for families who are seeking to develop spiritual practices within their family circle.

TOIYA WILLIAMS, Kids Director, The Summit Church

I walked away from *Building Spiritual Habits in the Home* with renewed energy and excitement for creating rhythms of worship in my ever-changing family. Chris and Clayton give fresh, grace-filled encouragement and so many practical tips for worn-out parents who really do want to establish spiritual habits in their homes, but just need some help . . . me included!

NATALIE ABBOTT, cofounder, Dwell Differently

This is an intensely practical book that I think has the potential to really equip families trying to disciple their children in gospel-centered ways. Many of our churches haven't done the greatest job "catechizing" our kids or building out a life-liturgy. But this book has the potential to help bridge that gap. It is filled with equal parts habit science and biblical truth—like a fusion between the practical insights of *Atomic Habits* and the sage wisdom of Eugene Peterson.

J. D. GREEAR, Lead Pastor, The Sur
author of *Gospel: Recovering the Powe*

T0284447

Building
Spiritual
Habits

in the
Home

Small Steps You
Can Take Today

CHRIS PAPPALARDO & CLAYTON GREENE

MOODY PUBLISHERS
CHICAGO

Edited by Philip F. Newman
Interior design: Puckett Smartt
Cover design: Brittany Schrock
Abstract grain texture copyright © 2024 by intenseartisan/Vecteezy. All rights reserved.

Library of Congress Cataloging-in-Publication Data

Names: Pappalardo, Chris, author. | Greene, Clayton, author.
Title: Building spiritual habits in the home : small steps you can take
   today / Chris Pappalardo and Clayton Greene.
Description: Chicago : Moody Publishers, [2025] | Includes bibliographical
   references. | Summary: "From good intentions to actual practice. Looking
   to the wisdom of Scripture, these dads teach you how to apply lasting
   faith practices to your family and your life. Are you ready? With just
   seven simple shifts to our spiritual habits, we can develop a spiritual
   life that will last!"-- Provided by publisher.
Identifiers: LCCN 2024031424 (print) | LCCN 2024031425 (ebook) | ISBN
   9780802434302 | ISBN 9780802470867 (ebook)
Subjects: LCSH: Families--Religious aspects--Christianity. |
   Spirituality--Christianity. | Christian life.
Classification: LCC BT707.7 .P36 2025 (print) | LCC BT707.7 (ebook) | DDC
   248.4--dc23/eng/20240909
LC record available at https://lccn.loc.gov/2024031424
LC ebook record available at https://lccn.loc.gov/2024031425

Originally delivered by fleets of horse-drawn wagons, the affordable paperbacks from D. L. Moody's publishing house resourced the church and served everyday people. Now, after more than 125 years of publishing and ministry, Moody Publishers' mission remains the same—even if our delivery systems have changed a bit. For more information on other books (and resources) created from a biblical perspective, go to www.moodypublishers.com or write to:

Moody Publishers
820 N. LaSalle Boulevard
Chicago, IL 60610

1 3 5 7 9 10 8 6 4 2

Printed in the United States of America

To Jenn and Kristen. Thank you for taking the small steps with us.

CONTENTS

The Hunt for Congruence

t all started when six-year-old Cara said, "Mommy and Daddy, you say that Christmas is all about Jesus, but it feels like Christmas is all about presents."

It was December 23, 2018. Christmas *fail*.

Fast-forward to November 2019. We had to find a solution, so we created Advent Blocks for our family and shared it with four others. One of those families was the Pappalardos. Chris Pappalardo is the author of *The King Is Coming*—our Advent Blocks guide—and the coauthor of this book.

Note: I (Clayton) am writing this introduction in my voice, while Chris will write the rest of the book in his voice, but we did all the work and writing together.

Cara's brutally honest comment sent Chris and me on a quest. We realized there was a gap between our stated intentions and our kids' lived experience. We were saying one thing and living another. And we wanted to figure out how to close that gap.

We didn't know it at the time, but we were on a hunt for *congruence*—a concept we first picked up from pastor and writer Eugene Peterson.[1] Congruence, Peterson said, describes the alignment between a pastor's words and his life. A pastor shouldn't just say what God wants him to say. A pastor should also live how God wants him to live. When the words and the life align, you get congruence.

What Peterson described for pastors, we began to apply to the family.

We believe there should be congruence between what we *say* we believe, what we *teach* our kids, and how we *live*. We got this idea (again, via Eugene

Peterson) by looking at the famous proverb: "Train up a child in the way he should go; even when he is old he will not depart from it" (Prov. 22:6). It doesn't say *teach* up your child. It says *train* up your child.

What sticks with this hypothetical child when he grows old is not a lesson learned in Sunday school. It's not a conversation shared around the dinner table. (Both of those matter, but something larger is at play here.) *We train our children with our entire lives.*

What we say, what we do, where we live, who we invite into our homes, how we spend our money, what we do with our free time—all of it trains up our children in certain ways.

Think about it this way: How many of our seven-year-olds have we taught, directly, to successfully navigate the landscape of our local Target? I'm guessing it's close to 0 percent. I know Chris and I haven't done it.

Second question: How many of those same seven-year-olds could, given the opportunity and a credit card, make their way into Target and come out with a box of Cinnamon Toast Crunch? Assuming they weren't stopped by a concerned stranger, I'm guessing it would be pretty close to 100 percent.

How did they learn this skill? We didn't *teach* them the way; we *trained* them in it. We did that training with countless trips to the store over time. My point here isn't to critique purchasing habits or even to weigh the pros and cons of Target. My point is simply this: We are training way more than we are teaching. So the best way to go about parenting is to train and teach in alignment.

We say we believe Jesus is better than anything life has to offer, but we get more excited about lounging at the pool than we do going to worship on a Sunday.

We say generosity is what God expects, but we build our shopping lists each month before giving to the poor or to our church.

We say God made us for community, but we would rather stay home and watch TV than have someone over for dinner.

We say, "Life doesn't happen on a screen," but then we lose ourselves, scrolling and scrolling and scrolling.

We teach and we train. And if they go against each other, the training is what will win.

That is what was so scary about Cara's comment. She was directly telling us that what we were saying was not lining up with how we were living. We lacked congruence. Yes, we were teaching her the real Christmas story. But we were training her up in Christmas presents more than we were training her in a Christian celebration.

The next year we went back to the drawing board. We wanted to teach *and* train. We wanted to bring our intentions closer to our family's experience. That process led us to join with a few other families and try a new type of Christmas tradition—one that combined experience and teaching.

Somehow, it worked.

That Christmas Eve, our girls were as excited about the story of Jesus as they were about the presents (though they were—and are—still very excited about the presents).

Clearly, something clicked.

So we reverse engineered what was working, applying the system to other areas of our lives where we wanted to train up our children—and ourselves. That has left us with some insights into how to create this alignment.

We think the principles we've stumbled upon are helpful for anyone who (1) wants to practice their faith and (2) feels like they're missing something. Because that's us, too.

A RUBRIC FOR TRAINING

Here are a few oversimplifications about Chris and me:

- I went to the University of North Carolina. He went to Duke. (Proof that unity in Christ is truly possible.)

- I have read a ton of habit-science books. He has read a ton of Bible.
- I love to make things practical. He loves to make things poetic.

Okay, so I may be exaggerating our differences a bit. But the main point is that we approach spiritual life and spiritual habits as complements to each other. Often, I'll walk in the room and ask Chris, "Why is X so hard? We should do more of that if we mean it." And he says, "Well, in the Bible, it says . . ." And we are off to the races solving a problem of congruence—in our lives and in the lives of our families as well.

What we have found is that the habit scientists are "discovering" truths that God has already beautifully put in place in the world. There is, so to speak, a great congruence between what James Clear says and what the Bible lays out.[2]

In this book, we've combined those principles so we could pass them along to you and your family. Because as different as Chris and I are, we share this in common: We deeply desire our children to know Jesus more personally every day. It's a desire I'm sure you share.

If you want more congruence in your life between what you say, what you believe, and how you live, join us. In this book you will find six small steps to help you develop spiritual habits in the home. When it comes to your spiritual habits, we believe you should (1) make it easy—easier than you think, (2) make it tangible, (3) pick a place, (4) choose your timing, (5) make it playful, and (6) find your friends.

But before we get too far ahead of ourselves trying to get good at our God habits, we need to know more about Him. We need to start with God.

That's where we begin. Chris, take it away . . .

First Things First

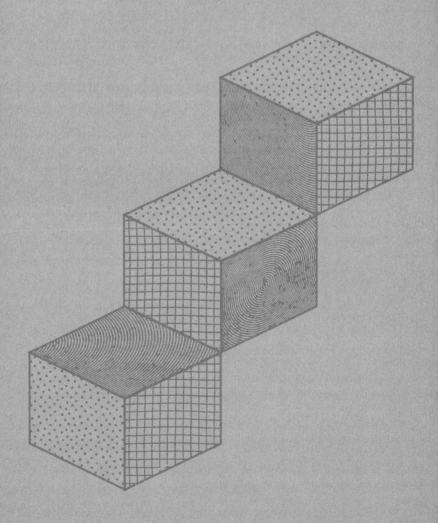

Who God Is

(and What That Means for
Your Spiritual Habits)

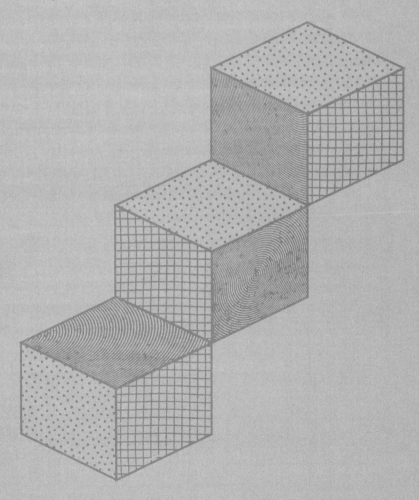

CHAPTER ONE

1. God starts.

2. God wants to be with you.

3. We can't see God, but He is there.

4. God prefers to work slowly.

5. God is gracious.

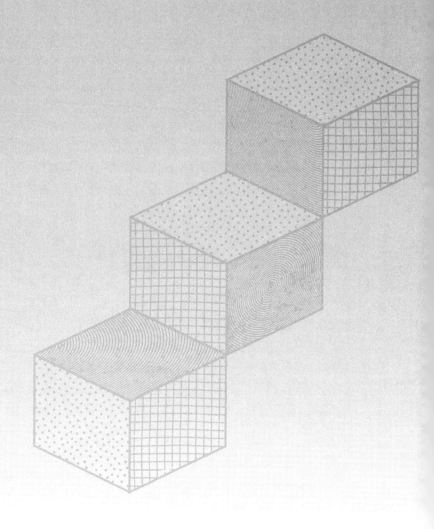

Learning from Peggy

As I stare out my kitchen window toward my backyard, my eye is naturally drawn to a gray and white dappled beech tree. In the summer, I'm thankful for the shade it provides. In the fall, I have more mixed feelings about it, as it deposits what feels like tens of thousands of leaves in my yard. Most of the time, though, I love this tree.

Because the beech tree dominates the backyard, my daughter, naturally, has named it—Peggy.

Farther back, through the woods, I can see another dozen of these beeches. Some of them have names, but most don't. The oldest of the bunch, by my estimation, is probably about fifty or sixty years old. As beech trees go, that's not terribly old. Beech trees are remarkable for their longevity, growing for hundreds of years. Some of the oldest beech trees in the United States are older than the country itself.

I think of this fact often, trying to imagine what life was like when Peggy was only a sapling. My house didn't exist. My neighborhood didn't exist. Hardly anybody I know existed.

Peggy's older relatives—her two-hundred-year-old cousins—grew up in a world of farmers and horse-drawn carriages, not airplanes and internet. Even "young" Peggy has lived through hundreds of freezing cold winter nights and just as many blazing hot summer days. Through it all, she doesn't seem any the worse for wear. Her only scar appears to be relatively recent—an emblem of the hopeful love of "KC + TL" etched in her trunk and surrounded by a heart.

Peggy reminds me that some of the most impressive change happens slowly, almost invisibly, over long periods of time. On any given day, I can walk outside and pull up a dozen small beech saplings without any effort. And I could have done that to Peggy at some point. But not in her present form. For me to take Peggy down now would require machinery roughly the size of my house. That's the power of slow, steady change.

When it comes to spiritual change, we should spend a lot more time trying to emulate Peggy.

FIVE ROOTS FOR OUR SPIRITUAL HABITS

Over the course of the following chapters, we're going to talk a lot about spiritual habits, offering small steps you can take to make your spiritual habits *stick*. But before we get to all of the steps, we need to make sure we've got our roots firmly planted in the soil. Like Peggy, our spiritual lives will never grow taller than our roots allow.

What are these spiritual "roots"? They are five fundamental truths about God, each of which should shape a healthy approach to your spiritual habits. These aren't necessarily the five most important truths about God—just the most relevant when we are thinking about how spiritual habits work.

Skip these five truths and you'll feel an ever-increasing weight on your already drooping shoulders. But ground your life in these truths, like roots embedded into the earth, and you'll find your spirit not only encouraged, but empowered to change.

Root 1: God Starts

From the first scene of the Bible ("In the beginning, God created...") to the last ("Come, Lord Jesus!"), God is the One setting the action in motion. In the lives of every saint in Scripture, God begins. He creates Adam and Eve. He calls Noah and Abraham and Moses. He rescues His people—from Egypt, from the Philistines, from themselves. In the life of Jesus, He chooses His twelve disciples. Through His Spirit, He sends out Paul and Barnabas. At no point in your Bible does a human being decide to go looking for God. God starts. Every. Single. Time.

This is also true of our spiritual stories. Whether you've been a Christian for fifteen minutes or fifty years, your story begins with the phrase, "In the beginning, God ..."

In the divine dance between you and God, God always plays the lead.

What does this mean for us and our spiritual habits?

So how does the truth that God starts (not us) shape our spiritual habits? Since He starts, our responsibility is to receive and respond. Spiritual life, like physical life, isn't something we earn or build. It's a gift. And the main thing you're supposed to do with a gift is receive it. God brings the initiative. We bring the open arms.

This runs against the grain of our hearts, which seem much more inclined to *work* our way to God. But the gospel message should destroy, every day, any sense of needing to climb a ladder to God's presence. When it comes to initiative, it's hard to imagine a more lopsided relationship! While we were far from God, He sent His Son, Jesus, to bring us back to Him. Jesus lived a perfect life, died for us, then rose from the dead.

And us? We don't do any of that. We simply believe and receive.

Once a person believes, of course, everything changes. Following Jesus means *doing* things. But at no point should our *doing* be confused with *earning*—or even initiating. God started this relationship. Every spiritual practice grows from the soil of God's initiating work. He speaks, we listen. He walks ahead, we follow. He calls, we respond.

Practically, this will mean that our spiritual habits are more open to God's leading, less fixed by our own disciplines. They may change as our season of life changes. They may look very different from one person to the next. God doesn't want all of us doing precisely the same habits. He wants all of us looking to Him, listening to Him, responding to Him. Since His conversation with each of us is unique, our responses will be, too.

I'll admit: Something about this thrills me and frightens me at the same time. It's thrilling to realize that God plays the lead in my spiritual habits. That really takes the pressure off. But it's scary, too, because I'm a big fan of control.

So to all of my fellow control addicts, and to myself, let's remember: God starts. He always has. And it's better that way.

Root 2: God Wants to Be with You

The primary tension in Scripture centers on this theme: God wants to be with His people. But again and again, something gets in the way. Adam and Eve, for instance, were personally created by God and lived with Him in the garden of Eden. But because of their sin, they were forced to leave. God, previously close enough to walk with them, now felt absent.

This problem persisted all throughout the Old Testament. In Noah's day, violence reigned because everyone forgot God. In Moses' day, God's people were enslaved, crying out to God for some kind of intervention—but He felt far off. In the days of the exile, God's people felt adrift, far from God and far from their home.

The central problem of the Bible echoes the central problem of many world religions: We sense, deep down, that God is out there. But something prevents us from actually connecting with Him.

What makes the biblical story beautiful, though, is how persistently God works to overcome this distance. The Bible is a chronicle of the many ways God chose to draw near to His people—through prophets, through dreams, in a pillar of fire, in the temple. And all of this culminates in Jesus, God in the flesh. Through the incarnation of Jesus, we see, once and for all, God's radical commitment to being with His people.

Jesus' life and ministry model this, too. Over and over again, the Gospels record Jesus' invitation for His followers to simply spend time with Him. "Come with me," He says to the disciples, "to a quiet place and get some rest" (Mark 6:31 NIV). His call might *end* by sounding like, "Do as I do." But it always *begins* with the much simpler invitation: "Be where I am."

What does this mean for us and our spiritual habits?

So how does the truth that God wants to be with us shape our spiritual habits? If the goal of our spiritual habits is spending time with Him, that provides a helpful unity to all of our spiritual disciplines. In prayer, I enter into a conversation with God. In silence, I listen for God's voice—or simply sit quietly knowing I sit *with* God. In reading my Bible, I remember that I'm not primarily trying to memorize facts, but to better know a person.

Seeing the goal of spiritual habits as communion with God also lowers the pressure we put on ourselves. For instance, if we think of spiritual habits primarily as tools to make us better people, then there's always a scoreboard looming over us. *Did I read enough chapters of the Bible this year? Did I pray long enough?* In this approach, the key word in our spiritual habits is that nasty one, "enough." Whether we're doing a little or doing a lot, it never feels like enough. The scoreboard keeps telling me I'm a loser.

Unless, of course, you've got a slightly different temperament. Maybe you're more naturally disciplined than others. You don't resent the scoreboard mentality. You relish it. This might feel nice for you, but it's not actually any better. Because while the scoreboard may be telling you that you're winning, it's not what Jesus is after.

Our spiritual habits aren't meant to make us feel like winners *or* like losers. They are meant to bring us closer to God, to know Him and open our hearts so we can experience His love. The goal is relationship—and in relationships, "winning" and "losing" aren't relevant categories. Intimacy is.

Root 3: We Can't See God, But He Is There

The third root might seem incredibly obvious to you, but we've found it influences our spiritual habits more than most people give it credit for. It's a truth that is simple and ancient and a little confusing: we can't see God, but He is there.

It might help to think about this one in conjunction with our second root—"God wants to be with you." It sounds really heartwarming that God wants to be with you. But you're smart enough to recognize it's not that simple. God isn't like us. We can't just invite Him over for dinner. Sure, there *was* a time when I could have found Him walking around and sharing meals with people. But that was two thousand years ago. Jesus isn't walking the streets of Raleigh, North Carolina, where I live. Not in the same way, anyway.

Even before Jesus, things seemed a bit simpler. For the ancient Jewish people, you could measure your nearness to God in geographic terms. God's presence dwelled in the temple: the closer to the temple, the closer to God. (We'll explore this idea a lot more in chapter 5. Hold tight.)

But for us today? The temple is gone. Jesus is gone. In their place, we have the Holy Spirit. Granted, Jesus said that having the Holy Spirit would be better than having Him stick around (John 16:7). And we believe Him. It *is* better. But it's also pretty confusing.

If God didn't exist, spending time with Him would be irrelevant. If God were confined to one physical location—a person or a temple, say—spending time with Him would be straightforward (though incredibly difficult to share). But God is real *and* God is invisible. We can't see God, but He is there.

What does this mean for us and our spiritual habits?

So what does this obvious and confusing truth mean for our spiritual habits? Three implications come to mind.

First, it reminds us that spiritual practices will often feel awkward. Relationships aren't easy anyway. But relationships with invisible people are bound to be even tougher. That's not to say we give up. It's simply to remind you that just because it's awkward doesn't mean you're doing it wrong.

Second, this truth reminds us about the importance of Christian community. God's Spirit may not be present the way He was in Jesus, but God's Spirit is still active today. The vehicle for God's Spirit, according to the apostle Paul, is the community of God (1 Cor. 12). We've felt this to be true: it's much easier to hear God's Spirit from others than from our own hearts. When a thought pops into my head, for instance, it *might* be from the Spirit, but I find it very easy to explain it away. But when my friend brings a word of encouragement or exhortation that resonates with what God has been teaching me, I sense that God really is speaking.

Third, this reminds us that much of the Christian life is about discernment. Since we can't see God, understanding where He is moving is not a scientific or straightforward process. It requires sensitivity and slowness—which is why many of the Christian spiritual disciplines involve slowing down. God invites us to discern what He is doing in the world. And the right spiritual habits can help us sharpen that discernment.

Root 4: God Prefers to Work Slowly

Most of us are fascinated with stories of God working miraculously and quickly, whether those stories are in Scripture or the lives of our friends. When God splits the Red Sea in a moment, our hearts leap. When Jesus heals paralytics and opens blind eyes, we wish we could be there to watch it happen. This is what we long for in our lives, in the lives of those we love. We want God to intervene in an instant, transforming us into who we ought to be. We want Him to kill the addiction, to restore the relationship, to heal our body. And we long for it to happen *fast*.

The trouble is, God rarely acts this way. God prefers a much slower method.

In his book *Three Mile an Hour God*, Japanese theologian Kosuke Koyama makes the case that God, by design, prefers to move at the speed of a walk—about three miles an hour. This is how Jesus operated in His ministry. He was never in a hurry. He lingered. Because He loved people deeply, He took His time with them.

God intends to radically change every one of us. In fact, He may change much more about us than we even anticipate. But He will also work much more subtly, much more slowly than most of us imagine. If we are to walk with God, we need to get used to walking at His pace.

What does this mean for us and our spiritual habits?

If God prefers slow work over rapid change, how does that shape our spiritual habits? It means we allow God to work at His pace—and we do our best to walk at that pace with Him.

Because God works slowly, we can forgive ourselves for not having it all together right now. God doesn't expect us to change in an instant. He's looking at a much longer timetable, and He's patient enough to soften our hearts over a lifetime.

Because God works slowly, we can celebrate small wins in the short term. You and I may be tempted to dismiss a small spiritual habit—say, reading a psalm a day—as insignificant. But walking at God's pace, we can celebrate that small step, just like a parent celebrates the first unsteady steps of their child.

And finally, because God works slowly we can recognize the beautiful invitation of rest inherent in so many of the traditional spiritual disciplines. Sabbath, for instance, is an invitation to slow down, enjoy God, and enjoy His world. Prayer is an invitation to slow down and know God. Our society may be filled with frantic demands to move faster, do more, achieve more. But the spiritual disciplines aren't like that at all. They offer our weary souls a place of rest.

Root 5: God Is Gracious

In his book *What's So Amazing About Grace?*, Philip Yancey records an anecdote from the life of C. S. Lewis:

During a British conference on comparative religions, experts from around the world debated what, if any, belief was unique to the Christian faith. They began eliminating possibilities. Incarnation? Other religions had different versions of gods appearing in human form. Resurrection? Again, other religions had accounts of return from death. The debate went on for some time until C. S. Lewis wandered into the room. "What's the rumpus about?" he asked, and heard in reply that his colleagues were discussing Christianity's unique contribution among world religions. Lewis responded, "Oh, that's easy. It's grace."[1]

We simply cannot overstate the importance of grace in the life of the Christian. God created us, even though He didn't need us (Gen. 1:26–28). That's grace.

God made Himself known to us, even though we weren't seeking Him (Isa. 65:1). That's grace.

God rescued us, even while we were His enemies (Rom. 5:10). That's grace.

God began His work in us before we knew it—or even wanted it (Eph. 1:3–10). That's grace.

God promises to finish His work in us (Phil. 1:6). That's grace.

God forgives us when we falter (Ex. 34:6–7a). That's grace.

God makes His very presence available to us (Isa. 41:10; Matt. 28:20). That's grace.

God gives us His Word to teach us, His Spirit to guide us, a community of faith to encourage us. That's grace, grace, grace.

From beginning to end, our spiritual lives dance along to the melody of amazing grace. Which means that God doesn't just *start*; because of His grace, He promises to *finish*, too.

When Jesus walked among us, He lived a life that the apostle John summarized as "full of grace and truth" (John 1:14). The truth piece is easy to recognize: You don't have to read long in the Gospels to see how fiery of a truth-teller Jesus could be! His sermons cut people to the heart, often infuriating them—especially the religious leaders. But the heart of Jesus overflows with grace. Over and over again, Jesus invited people in. To the broken, the sinful, the outcast, He said, "Come to me."

Jesus' gracious heart shows us the heart of God. This was the same God who, when Moses met Him on the mountain, announced Himself as "the LORD, the LORD, a God merciful and gracious" (Ex. 34:6). God lists several other attributes after this, but it is no accident that the first two He mentions are *mercy* and *grace*. This is who God is.

If we are to follow Jesus, we walk not only at His pace; we walk in His grace.

What does this mean for us and our spiritual habits?

So how does God's grace shape our spiritual habits? Simply this: It changes the tenor and tone of our attempts. Since God is gracious to us, we can feel the freedom to fail. Since God is gracious to us, we can return to Him after long gaps in our spiritual practice. Since God is gracious to us, we can always, always, *always* try again.

Just think: How would Jesus respond to your failures if He were here in the flesh right now—if He found out, for instance, that you hadn't prayed for a month, or that you forgot to read your daughter her nighttime Bible story for ten straight days (or that you've never even *thought* to do that)? He wouldn't scowl at you and demand you do better. He would invite you in. He would open his arms to you. In grace, He would simply say, "Come to me."

Spiritual life—and the habits that flow from it—doesn't have to feel like a bunch of homework you're always behind on. Experiencing spiritual life that way can feel like holding your breath through some hard exercise or experience. Do you know that feeling of gutting out your Bible reading or prayer? It can feel like being underwater, starving for air.

But realize that God is abundantly gracious, and suddenly your spiritual life can feel more like breathing after you've been holding your breath for far too long.

That's how we view spiritual habits, and how we'd encourage you to view them, too—as the *inhale and exhale* of a healthy spiritual life. Throughout this book, we're going to encourage you to focus on *one* spiritual habit. Just one. Which one should you pick? And what is a spiritual habit anyway?

So glad you asked.

What Is a Spiritual Habit, Anyway?

CHAPTER TWO

At the core of every spiritual habit is this reality:

Respond to God by paying attention . . . at His pace, and in His grace.

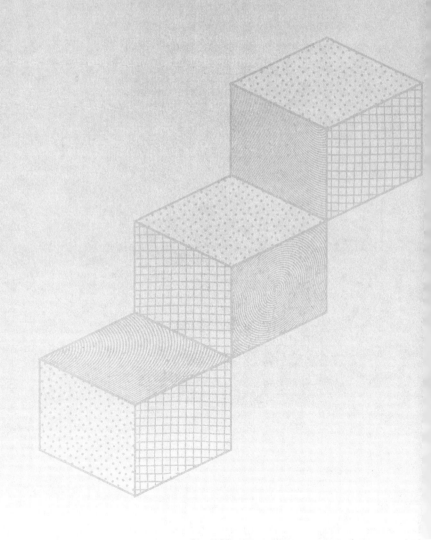

The Garden Snail

When my son Teddy was three years old, there was a little rhyme he loved. I would make my hand into a "snail" by balling it up into a fist and having my thumb act as the snail's head. With excruciating slowness, this "snail" would crawl from Teddy's toes up to his head, while I said: "Slowly, slowly, very slowly, creeps the garden snail. Slowly, slowly, very slowly up the garden rail."

It was the second part, though, that he was waiting for. Suddenly the "snail" would turn into a "mouse" and scurry all over him: "Quickly, quickly, very quickly, runs the little mouse. Quickly, quickly, very quickly, all around the house!" I would tickle him until he exploded with giggles, eventually laughing so hard he'd get the hiccups (something he inherited from me).

What made the rhyme fun for my son is just how long it took to get to "the good part." The whole time that snail was crawling—slowly, slowly, very slowly—Teddy's eyes would widen because he knew it was headed somewhere. At no other moment in his little life, before or since, has he been able to sit and wait so well.

Waiting is tough work, whether you're three or thirty-three. Waiting for the last day of school. Waiting for an answer to your many job applications. Waiting for your kid's fever to break. Waiting for the results from your unexpected biopsy.

Waiting for God to answer your deep, vulnerable, secret prayer.

Throughout Scripture, God's people frequently find themselves in a place of waiting. Think of Abraham and Sarah, for instance, who were promised a son, only to wait years for God to fulfill that promise. Think of Moses, who was promised to become the liberator of his nation, but who heard Pharaoh's voice, again and again, say, "I will not let this people go." Think of David, who was anointed king but had to wait over a decade before he was crowned—much of that time running for his life and hiding in caves.

Or think of Jesus' disciples, who had to wait several years to even figure out what His kingdom was truly about.

As we mentioned in the last chapter, *God prefers to work slowly*. For each of these people, God delivered on His promise. But He did it like the garden snail—slowly, slowly, very slowly.

We're often tempted to confuse God's slowness with God's absence. But the apostle Peter reminds us that God's pace is for our good: "The Lord is not slow to fulfill his promise as some count slowness, but is patient toward you, not wishing that any should perish, but that all should reach repentance" (2 Peter 3:9). In other words, God is not slow. Not really. He is patient. He walks with us and works with us *at His pace*, and that pace itself is a mark *of His grace.*

The Christian life is often not as fast as we'd like. But it will come more surely than we can imagine. Surely, surely, slow and surely—this is the environment of our spiritual life.

SLOWLY AND SURELY: DEFINING "SPIRITUAL HABIT"

We believe that our spiritual habits should flow from this combination of slowness and sureness—which you might recognize as echoes of the five roots we talked about in chapter 1. In fact, our entire view of spiritual habits should grow out of those five roots.

Let's look at those roots again, making them a little more simple and memorable:

1. **God starts.** We don't need to feel the burden of initiating in our spiritual habits. Which means our first action is always a response.

2. **God wants to be with you.** The goal of any spiritual habit isn't achievement, but intimacy. Which means we seek not just to understand spiritual stuff, but to know God.

3. **You can't see God, but He is there.** We aren't charting the course of our spiritual habits alone. Which means we have to cue ourselves to God's presence and work in our lives.

4. **God prefers to work slowly.** God is patient with you as you stumble along. Which means spiritual habits can feel frustrating and slow.

5. **God is gracious.** Our spiritual habits are bathed in grace and mercy and forgiveness. His work in our lives is more sure than we could imagine. Which means we can expect to fail and feel the invitation to start over, again and again and again.

Given all that, what is our responsibility in our spiritual habits?

We (step 1) respond to a God who wants to know us by (step 2) cuing ourselves to pay attention to His presence and work in our lives.

Or, to boil it down even more: We *respond* to God and *pay attention* to His presence.

We respond.

We pay attention.

And all of this happens in God's rhythm of slowness and sureness—at His pace and in His grace. Slower than we might like, but more sure than we can imagine.

Think of your spiritual life as a garden (I'm taking my lead here from Jesus in John 15). A good garden grows and eventually bears fruit. But how? Consider each element of our definition:

1. *Respond to a God who wants to know you.* For a garden to flourish, we need much more than good seeds. We need good soil. You and I are plants (like Peggy), but we can't just put down roots wherever we want. Our life begins when we plant ourselves in the soil of God's activity. *God starts.* God is the soil, the only environment in which our spiritual lives make sense. The life

of a plant comes from its connection to the soil. Cut off a branch, no matter how beautiful, and that branch is already essentially dead. As Jesus put it, our goal is to "abide" in Him, to be connected to Him.

2. *Pay attention to His presence.* Much of what makes gardening maddening (to me, anyway) is adjusting your care of the plants. We don't just pick good seed, plant it in good soil, and then wait. No, we tend the garden—watering, weeding, fertilizing, pruning. But the best gardeners know you don't just do all of these practices every time. You have to pay attention to the garden to know what kind of tending is best. So in our spiritual life, we choose practices that allow us to pay attention to God's work in our lives.

3. *At His pace and in His grace.* We can't rush the growth of a seed. Fertilizer may make the growth faster, but a growing plant is never *fast.* Some seasons are ripe for growth. In other seasons, the plant focuses more on its roots, hardly growing visibly at all. In every season, we wait for a process that is as beautiful as it is slow. Then, when the seed finally does sprout from the soil, we feel a thrill of gratitude. Sure, we did our work, but we didn't make the plant grow. God did. A flower is a gift of grace. And so is a flowering spiritual life.

Disciplines or Practices or Habits? (And Does It Even Matter?)

You may have noticed that we've already used several phrases to talk about "spiritual habits" in the home. There are actually a number of ways to talk about these realities, each of which has its own benefits—and drawbacks.

Why we like (and don't like) the phrase "spiritual practice":

- Like it: Practice carries feelings of amateur status—the root for "amateur" meaning, literally, someone who does something because they *love* it. None of us are experts. All of us can practice.

- Don't like it: Practice can often feel like pressure. For many of us, "practice" conjures homework lessons we have to do, rather than something fun we get to do.

Why we like (and don't like) the phrase "spiritual life":

- Like it: Truly, all of life *is* spiritual. We believe everything we do can be a form of spiritual engagement.
- Don't like it: "Spiritual life" feels a bit squishy at times. It doesn't quite capture the idea that there are still certain things God would like us to do—or do differently.

Why we like (and don't like) the phrase "spiritual rhythm":

- Like it: Rhythms feel very gracious. They change over time and according to the season.
- Don't like it: A lot of our spiritual life happens in a rhythmic pattern, but not all of it.

Why we like (and don't like) the phrase "spiritual discipline":

- Like it: You need to regularly engage. You have to regularly weed the garden, for instance. And "discipline" is right there in that world. Plus, it's probably the most commonly used and familiar phrase.
- Don't like it: If "practice" feels like pressure, "discipline" can feel like drudgery. A disciplined person works hard and expects results. But it's easy to miss the God-initiated and Spirit-led element here.

Why we like (and don't like) the phrase "spiritual habits":

- Like it: Most of what shapes our lives happens because of our habits. Plus, thinking in terms of habits allows us to apply what experts say from the field of habit science (which we find very fruitful).
- Don't like it: Habits can become so regimented that they become cold and leave little room for us to pay attention to God's new or surprising interactions.

Throughout this book, we'll use the phrase "spiritual habits" most often. But we don't want you to get hung up on terminology. We'll even bounce around from phrase to phrase through the book. If you really love one of these other phrases, know that we love it, too.

The key element here isn't just the words we're using, but the approach we're taking. Are we approaching the habits (or disciplines or practices) from a posture of grace or from a posture of performance? When you feel the tension in this process, go back to the five roots from chapter 1. And remember, *God wants to be with you*. That's the goal.

WHAT WE'RE AFTER ARE GRACE-FILLED HABITS

I like the image of the garden because it captures a bit of a dance between two very different ideas—grace and habit. That may seem like an odd pair, but it's a beautiful one. It's like peanut butter and chocolate: When H. B. Reese floated the idea of a peanut butter-chocolate candy in 1928, the bigwigs at Hershey told him it would never work. Nearly a century later, Reese's peanut butter cups continue to dominate. Odd pairings can work.

Like grace and habit. Together, they provide the exact nuance we need in our spiritual life. Either one without the other will torpedo our attempts to grow. If we focus on habits without grace, our spiritual habits easily become duties and achievements. Pride wins. But if we only think about grace and never look at our habits, we won't actually be motivated to change. Inertia wins.

What we're after, then, is a fusion of mercy and movement, of doing and not-doing. It's what we like to call *grace-filled habits*. *Grace* reminds us that God is the one who does the work. (That plant won't come up unless God gives the growth.) *Habit* reminds us that God chooses to do that work *in* us and *through* us. (We've got some watering to do!)

Changing habits isn't easy. So it's important to remember that as we're walking with Jesus, none of us are high achievers. And that's okay. We may start a spiritual discipline, then muddle through for a while. Then we fall out of the habit, and begin again. This whole process is okay, because we're walking with Jesus—at *His pace,* and in *His grace.*

Grace-filled habits flow from the reality that *God wants to be with you.* He's after a relationship with you—and relationships come with their own sets of rhythms. Think of a marriage relationship, for instance. In a healthy marriage, a husband and wife will regularly find time to get away for date nights. That consistent habit is part of the relationship. But more importantly, that habit *feeds* the relationship.

It's important that we keep the relational side of things in view as we get going. Because throughout this book, we'll use all kinds of illustrations and applications from the habit scientists, as well as from our own lives—about gardening, or working out, or eating better, or reading more. And if we're not careful, a lot of these illustrations can make you think that performance is the goal.

It's not. Performance is not the goal here. Connection is. Remember, *God wants to be with you.* Grace-filled habits provide a way to cultivate that connection. They're not the goal; they're just the vehicle. They give us an opportunity to notice what God is doing and join Him in it.

A few years ago, our friend Brian was walking to school with two of his kids, who were in first and fourth grade. It wasn't an exceptional day. No one had a big test coming up or a vacation the family was anticipating. Just a normal, Tuesday-morning, ten-minute walk to school.

Until, as they approached the school, his first grader walked a little closer to Brian, reached out, and took his hand. Then the fourth grader did, too. And for a brief moment, the three of them walked, holding hands, just as they had when the kids were toddlers.

Brian's experience that day captures a bit of the feeling we are praying for you—not just healthy spiritual habits, but opportunities for renewed connection. For Brian, walking to school was the habit. It provided the opportunity. But what made that day worth remembering? Not the habit, but the connection.

That's what we're after. And that's what the spiritual habits are for.

SPIRITUAL HABITS: A FEW OF OUR FAVORITES

Let's take a quick look at some of our favorite spiritual habits, so you can see how our definition of spiritual habit applies to each one.

1. Bible Reading: A Habit That Helps You Know God

Respond to a God who wants to know you. God chose to make Himself known to us, and the vehicle He chose for that was a book. (We might have preferred a podcast or an Instagram reel. But the book is what we've got.) God writing a book is tremendously good news. It means, like we've mentioned, that *God starts.* We don't have to go searching for clues about His will for our lives. He has already made that known. We don't have to guess what God thinks. He's told us.

Pay attention to His presence. If we are asking ourselves to pay attention to what God is doing in our lives, there is no better place to start than His Word. Joining Him in His story *today* requires that we know the story that has preceded us. Can you imagine an actor trying to come into the second act of a play without having seen or read the script from the first?

At His pace and in His grace. Jesus taught His disciples over the course of three years. He taught as He went, circling back to many of the same stories and themes multiple times. As we read God's words in the Bible, we don't need to be in a rush. He intends for us to spend our whole lives learning. You never really *finish* reading the Bible. And that's totally okay.

2. Prayer: A Habit to Help You Discern God's Voice

Respond to a God who wants to know you. Prayer is a conversation with God. But the first word in that conversation doesn't come from our lips; it comes from God's heart. The best prayer, then, begins with listening or reading. In prayer, we learn to have a conversation with God, responding to what He has told us, asking Him for what we need, sharing our struggles with Him.

Pay attention to His presence. Talking to someone who is not physically present can be hard to remember. And even if you *do* remember, it probably feels really awkward. One theologian compares prayer to being in the middle of the woods and trying to find your way out by listening for the sound of tires rolling over gravel on the nearest dirt road.[1] Paying attention is pivotal.

At His pace and in His grace. Relationships can't be rushed. Over the course of your lifetime, God will have thousands of things He wants to say to you. And you'll have thousands of things to share with Him, too. Walking at His pace, you won't feel the need to pack all of that in one prayer session. Nor will you feel the pressure to make every prayer session feel the same. Praying in grace means we see all the many types of prayer as invitations, not obligations. Choose one and pray as you can, letting go of expectations for all the ways you *aren't* praying.

3. Sabbath: A Habit That Slows You Down

Respond to a God who wants to know you. After creating the universe, God rested on the seventh day (Gen. 2:2–3). Then He invited us into that same rhythm of work and rest. We don't rest primarily because we're tired. We rest because we are responding in gratitude to a God who has provided for us. From the very beginning, Sabbath has been a "get to" invitation in the midst of a "have to" world. It's an invitation, one day a week, to stop all of our good work so we can enjoy all of God's good work—and in that enjoyment, get to know the heart of God.

Pay attention to His presence. The 24/7 life of our contemporary world won't let you slow down, even for a moment. Resting one day out of seven is a profoundly countercultural act, which means we need major help doing it. To pay attention to this habit, we need something—or several somethings—that will stop us in our tracks.

At His pace and in His grace. Sabbath leans into "at His pace" more than any other spiritual habit. Our world wants us to move faster, always doing more, buying more, achieving more. Sabbath pushes the other way, reminding us that a life of joy and celebration doesn't happen at top speed. It happens when we slow our pace to a walk.

Vacation: A Habit We Made Up (Kinda)

Respond to a God who wants to know you. God made us to rest in Him. Sabbath was so central to following Him that it was the first practice He instituted. In fact, He actually instituted *several* kinds of Sabbaths, even year-long ones called "Jubilees" (we'll get more into that in chapter 6). Rest is a habit that matters a lot to God. So shouldn't rest be a key element of our spiritual lives? True, God never goes on vacation. But wherever you're going for vacation, God went first. And often, if you're like me, you're actually more aware of God on vacation than you are during your normal life rhythms.

Pay attention to His presence. Vacation helps us pay attention in a world that is overly consumed by work and working. The "win" with vacation may not be coming away with a new realization about God. More likely, it will be in carving out time to pay attention to key people in your life. But those people are God's gift to you. Knowing them and being known by them is valuable indeed.

At His pace and in His grace. When God's people were enslaved in Egypt, they never had the opportunity to rest. Vacations weren't an option. Very few of us live in that kind of enforced tyranny. And yet, we often choose to overwork rather than pausing to rest and connect. If we believe God is gracious toward us, one way we will show it is by going on vacation.

4. Hospitality: A Habit That Puts You in Community

Respond to a God who wants to know you. We often think of spiritual habits as solo endeavors—and some spiritual habits are—but one of the best ways for us to engage with God is by engaging with other people. God created Adam, then declared that it was not good for Adam to be alone. So He created the first human community by making Eve. Relationships are not an accident of our fallen nature or a necessary element of being weak. They are God's idea.

Pay attention to His presence. Our initial experience in most relationships centers on how those relationships are affecting us. People are annoying us or, on the other hand, making us feel welcome and seen. But in any relationship, God intends to grow us to become more like Him. The trouble is, we struggle to recognize the work God wants to do in us through these people. Sharing a meal together is a great way to see into each other's lives so that we can encourage and correct and care.

At His pace and in His grace. Hospitality isn't easy because people aren't easy. It takes a long time to know others and be known by them. Along the way, you'll hurt people you love and be hurt by them. God wants us to lean into all of this mess, because God wants us to become people of compassion. We can't do it without God's grace. But thankfully, that grace is always abundant and available.

SPIRITUAL HABITS: A BUFFET OF CHOICES

Alright, so much for the big ones. Let's show you a few more.

In the chapters to come, we're going to encourage you to pick *one* spiritual habit you'd like to grow in. Maybe you already found your one. (If it's "vacation," more power to you.) If not, to help you choose, we've provided a longer list. Consider this your buffet of spiritual habits.

Now, remember, the goal here isn't to heap all of these on you. It's to help you see the full buffet so you can put *one* thing on your plate. You can always start this process over with another spiritual habit. But for now, just choose one.

We've grouped the spiritual habits into four major categories—habits that (1) help you know God, (2) put you in community, (3) adjust your pace, or (4) help you discern direction. (A lot of these habits could have shown up in multiple categories. So don't take the classification too strictly.) Our hope is that if you're unsure which spiritual habit to have in mind as you read the following chapters, these categories can help you narrow it down.

1. Habits to Help You Know God

If you want know God better, try one of these:

- **Bible Reading** – As we mentioned above, God chose to reveal Himself to us through a book. To understand Him more, start there.
- **Prayer** – Prayer isn't just a way for us to tell God what's going on in our lives. It's a conversation. If you want to connect more with God, lean into the conversation.
- *Lectio Divina* – Latin for "spiritual reading," *lectio divina* is simply a type of Bible reading that encourages slowness and reflection. Choose just a verse or two, take your time pondering them, and listen for God's insights.
- **Fasting** – Fasting involves intentionally skipping a meal (or several) in order to spend that time remembering   and feeling—this truth: "Man does not live by bread alone, but man lives by every word that comes from the mouth of the LORD" (Deut. 8:3).

2. Habits That Put You in Community

If you want a spiritual habit with a community element, try one of these:

- **Hospitality** – Open up your home to those who would not normally be there. The most common way to do this is to invite someone in for a meal.
- **Generosity** – Regularly give away some of your resources, mirroring the generosity of God. This is easiest for us to apply to money, but can just as easily apply to our time or our attention.
- **Service** – Choose a volunteer opportunity, whether through your church or another organization, to provide a tangible benefit to people in need.
- **Worship** – Attend a worship service, which combines several spiritual habits all at once. Particularly unique here is the opportunity to

sing together—which, according to Andy Crouch, allows us to love God with our heart, soul, mind, *and* strength.[2]

- **Conversation** – Our friend Justin Whitmel Earley encourages the spiritual discipline of leisurely, vulnerable conversation among friends. For him, the target is one hour a week.

3. Habits That Adjust Your Pace

If you feel like you need to adjust the pace of your life (and who doesn't?), try one of these:

- **Sabbath** – For one day a week, stop all of your work so you can enjoy all of God's works. Sabbath is celebration and rest, both of which God graciously wants to give to you.
- **Silence and Solitude** – These two distinct practices often go together. In silence, you intentionally avoid talking or hearing from others. To achieve this, you need solitude, where you remove yourself, for a time, from the company of others. Together, silence and solitude allow you to still the noise around you and within you so you can better hear God's voice.
- **Vacation** – Take several days away from your work and (preferably) from your home so you can rest and enjoy time with others. Bonus points if nature is involved.
- **Gratitude** – Write down prayers of thanksgiving to God, regularly coming up with multiple reasons to say "thank you"—even if the items are small.

4. Habits That Help You Discern Direction

If you are in need of discernment and direction, try one of these.

- **Listening Prayer** – Read Scripture and pray, but leave time and space for God to guide you as you engage in these practices. Rather than merely talking to God, ask Him for His wisdom.

- **Confession** – Both to God and to a trusted friend, acknowledge what is sinful in your life and receive God's forgiveness.
- **Journaling** – Write down your prayers, your reflections on Scripture, or your own feelings. Writing is slow, but it allows you to synthesize what is going on in your heart and mind. It also helps you retain lessons you've learned.
- **Examen** – Every evening (or every morning), slowly replay the past day, focusing on moments where your emotions were most heightened. For all that was good, thank God for His goodness and His presence. For all that was hard, bring it to God, remembering that He was present with you then, too.

Write the one spiritual habit you are choosing to focus on for now:

Six Small Steps

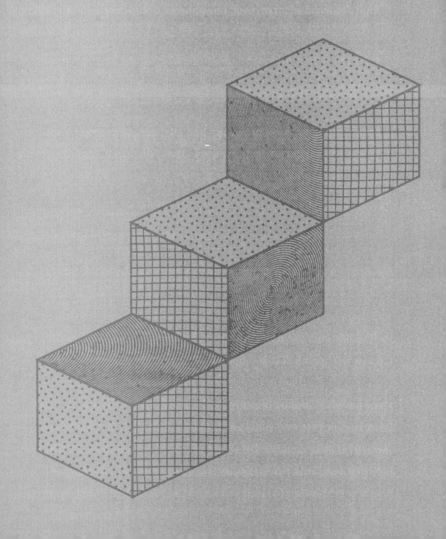

Make It Easy

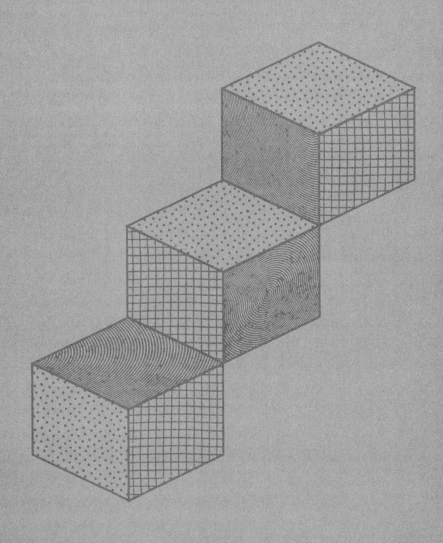

CHAPTER THREE

Question: Can you accomplish (or at least start) the habit in five minutes or less?

Our "small step" suggestion: Make a clear and easy plan—something you can start in five minutes or less.

1. **Forgive yourself:** Don't listen to influencers (much).
2. **Make it easier than you think:** Don't just start with easy. Start with easier—much easier—than you think you need to.
3. **Write it down:** Decide up front on the what, the where, the when, the who.

Anybody Hungry?

t's noon on a Friday. You're with a group of friends, trying to pick a restaurant. Everyone is already on the brink of hangry. (At least . . . hungr-irritable?) The following discussion ensues:

> **Steve**: Okay, here are the options: We've got *Pie Are Squared*, the new pizza place. Then there's *How Now Chow Chow*? I love their Tokyo Bowl. Ooh! There's also *Nic Cage Free Eggs*, that brunch spot Nicolas Cage opened downtown.
>
> **Amy**: Eh, I'm not really in the mood for pizza.
>
> **Ethan**: Yeah, me neither. Plus, *How Now* doesn't really have any gluten-free options.
>
> **Kristen**: And Nic Cage is overrated.[1]
>
> **Steve**: [*Stomach grumbles.*]

You ever been there? Hungry, annoyed, and *stuck*? In the end, it's no surprise when you end up at Chipotle. (Which, hey, there are worse things. But still.)

Making decisions in a group is tricky. But what many of us don't realize is that we've got a bunch of "Steves" and "Kristens" in our own minds. Every time we try to start a new habit, we start arguing with ourselves. And more often than not, we end up back where we started—stuck.

Decisions don't have to be huge to be hard. They just have to be new, because new is difficult. So if you're looking to start a new habit (or kick an old one), you've got to figure out what to do with Kristen and Steve.

You've got to make things much, much simpler.

WHAT YOU'RE FEELING HAS A NAME: DECISION FATIGUE

What you're feeling in that moment of indecision has a name. Psychologists call it "decision fatigue."[2] Maybe you've heard the phrase. You've definitely felt the reality.

Imagine a gas tank in your brain, filled with "decision fuel." It gets filled up while you sleep, so you start the day full (ish). Throughout the day, every new decision you make burns a little fuel.

What should I wear to work? *Burn.*

What shoes go with this outfit? *Burn.*

What should I have for breakfast? *Burn.*

And that's just the preliminary stuff. Throughout your actual day, you're burning through this decision fuel like crazy. If you're working, this is the mental energy you burn to get everything done. If you're watching kids, the pistons are firing every moment they're awake (and, let's be honest, when they're asleep, too).

By day's end, you're likely to be running on fumes. Which can make dinner time with three little kids a picture of pandemonium. If you're asking, "What should I make for dinner?" at five, while Charlie is dumping his school bag on the kitchen floor and Ella is screaming at you from the bathroom to "*Wipe me-e-e-e-e!*" you're not likely to have your best decision-making abilities at the ready.

And here's something that makes it even more tricky: Small decisions seem to burn through your fuel just as easily as big ones. Something as small as having to choose your kid's outfit at seven a.m. makes it harder to decide how to respond to a weeping coworker at three p.m.

This all sounds a bit fatalistic. But it's not as bad as you might think. Most of us, intuitively, know how to limit our decision fatigue: We make fewer choices. Sometimes we do it on purpose. Sometimes it kinda just happens. Either way, most of our day isn't a result of conscious decisions, but a result of ingrained habits. We run on autopilot.[3]

Just think about it: There are probably two or three viable ways for you to drive to your office every morning. But chances are, you take the same route every day. Most mornings, you glide into your favorite spot without really registering that you were driving at all. It just, well, happened.

Most of the time, reverting to autopilot serves us well. We don't usually expend decision energy asking, "How do I get to work?" or "Which side of the bed will I sleep on tonight?" Those autopilot "decisions" leave fuel in the tank for real choices.

The trouble comes when we want something in our lives to change. Picking up a new habit takes us off of autopilot. It slows us down. Now we're actively making decisions, burning through that fuel, and it gets tiring in a hurry. The more choices you have to make, the harder it is to push through. The easier it is to quit.

Which is what many of us end up doing.

YOU AREN'T AS LAZY AS YOU THINK

When you're on the cusp of quitting—or giving up before you start—it's easy to shift the focus away from the task and onto you. You might begin by feeling something like, *Wow, this sure is new, and new is hard!* But most of us quickly transition to something like, *This is just too much for me; I'm not cut out for this.* Or, *Other people can do this and it seems easy for them. I must not have what it takes. I'm too lazy.*

Maybe you're lazy. But it's more likely you're stuck. As James Clear puts it in *Atomic Habits*, "Many people think they lack motivation when what they really lack is clarity."[4] We're quick to moralize our failed attempts to change. Christians may be particularly susceptible to this. We think, *Good people make good changes and lazy people don't.* But that's not usually true—and it's hardly ever helpful.

In *Switch*, Chip and Dan Heath point out, "What looks like resistance [to change] is often a lack of clarity."[5] We might add: What looks like lack of faith or laziness is often confusion. We don't need to beat ourselves up for our horrible habits. We need a crystal clear path, one that uses up as little of our "decision fuel" as possible.

Most of the books we've read about decision fatigue end up pointing toward being more productive. As a pair of Enneagram Type 3s (yes, we went there), Clayton and I love productivity. But we aren't really concerned with productivity here. What we want is a kick start to our spiritual habits. And we believe thinking about decision fatigue shows us a clue.

Trying something new breaks our autopilot and forces us to use our "decision fuel." So if we're going to make it last, we need to get all the deciding out of the way *before* we start. We need to make that first step *easy*, knowing that even the easiest step is going to burn through more fuel than you're used to. And not just easy, but ridiculously easy. Far easier than you think it needs to be.

To which you might say, "Wait just a minute . . . should Christianity even be easy?" We're so glad you asked.

THE "EASY" CHRISTIAN LIFE

We aren't the first ones to suggest that the Christian life could be easy. Take it from Jesus Himself:

> "Come to me, all who labor and are heavy laden, and I will give you rest. Take my yoke upon you, and learn from me, for I am gentle and lowly in heart, and you will find rest for your souls. For my yoke is easy, and my burden is light." (Matt. 11:28–30)

Now, to be clear, this is also the same guy who just a few verses earlier told His followers, "I am sending you out as sheep in the midst of wolves" (Matt. 10:16), "You will be hated by all for my name's sake" (Matt. 10:22), and "Whoever does not take his cross and follow me is not worthy of me" (Matt. 10:38). So He's clearly not promising a life of carefree ease. Following Jesus is hard. It requires complete surrender. It reorients everything about our lives. It is costly.

And yet, at the same time, we want to take Jesus at His word: He said He had an "easy" yoke for us. He said He was bringing rest for weary souls, not more homework for those of us failing class.

So what gives?

Think about the "yoke" metaphor. A yoke is a wooden beam placed on a pair of oxen, helping them pull in the same direction. It's a tool for work. Jesus doesn't promise that following Him gets us out of the yoke. He promises a *different* yoke—an easy one rather than a burdensome one.

As a contrast, consider Jesus' words later in Matthew about the religious leaders of His day: "The scribes and the Pharisees . . . tie up heavy burdens, hard to bear, and lay them on people's shoulders, but they themselves are not willing to move them with their finger" (Matt. 23:2, 4). Rather than offering people a light burden and an easy yoke, the religious leaders created heavy burdens and a hard yoke: Give more money, pray longer prayers.

When Jesus said, "Follow me," He wasn't simply asking us to believe a few things about Him. He was inviting us into a way of life. That way of life—that "yoke"—is something we not only (1) practice for ourselves, but also (2) promote for the people around us. So it's not a question of *if* we're placing yokes on the shoulders of others. It's a question of *what kind* of yoke we're placing on them. The Pharisees opted for the heavy yoke. Jesus offers a lighter one.

I'm sure you've felt a heavy religious yoke, whether it's one you placed on yourself or—just as likely—one placed on you by others. The yoke of the Pharisees still hangs over many of us. So when someone becomes a Christian, they suddenly feel intense pressure to perform. Whether overtly or subtly, they hear a voice telling them, "Welcome to the family! Now, you've got a lot of work to do. You need to tell someone in your office about Jesus every other day. You need to read the Bible for forty-five minutes every morning. You need to pray—that means talking out loud to someone you can't see—for another fifteen minutes. Oh, and let's have a look at your finances, because you need to start giving a lot of that away, too. Don't worry, we've got a whole chart."

Does that sound like an easy yoke?

Following Jesus isn't always easy—if by "easy" we mean without effort and without cost. But following Jesus can be *easier than we usually make it*. I'm convinced that a lot of the burden we're carrying here isn't a result of following Jesus. After all, *God is gracious*. If we're following Jesus, we're doing it *at His pace* and *in His grace*. Growth is slower than we might like, but more certain than we can imagine. Slow, certain . . . and yes, easy.

A heavy yoke isn't "gospel"—that is, "good news"—to anyone receiving it. It's discouraging for the strongest of us, and downright crushing for the weakest.

THE RADICAL DEMOCRACY OF CHRISTIANITY

Speaking of weak, there's one more reason the "easy yoke" matters: It's what we like to call the "radical democracy" of Christianity.

We've already looked at Jesus critiquing the Pharisees' "heavy burden" from Matthew 23. Consider the parallel account in Luke's gospel:

> "Beware of the scribes, who like to walk around in long robes, and love greetings in the marketplaces and the best seats in the synagogues and the places of honor at feasts, *who devour widows' houses* and for a pretense make long prayers. They will receive the greater condemnation." (Luke 20:46–47, emphasis added)

We tend to imagine the Pharisees as self-righteous, overly religious people. That was certainly part of the problem, but it's not the entire critique Jesus lobs at them here. What He says—and this is no accident—is that they "devour widows' houses." Their heavy burdens were uniquely crushing for those with the least ability to carry them—widows.

Throughout Scripture, widows (along with orphans, immigrants, and the poor) exemplified helplessness. The Old Testament repeatedly presents God as someone who defends these helpless groups, calling God's people to do the same. God's kingdom was not to be built like the other kingdoms of the world, where only the best and brightest were rewarded. In God's kingdom, *everyone* was invited to sit at the King's table. It was—and is—the most radically democratic invitation the world has ever known.

Jesus' ministry followed this pattern. He was always angling toward the helpless, the sick, the outsiders. They all had a seat at His table. But the Pharisees? They were devouring not just the widow's table, but her entire house.

When it comes to spiritual habits, many people in our churches are just like those widows. They sense that they should be trying really hard for God, but they struggle to find their footing. They're more familiar with the yoke of the Pharisees than the yoke of Jesus. And their shoulders can't carry the load.

But remember what we said in chapter 2: The point of our spiritual habits is not to *perform* for God but to be *with* God. "Being with" is something that all people are capable of. Which means that when we paint the vision of the model Christian life, it ought to look like something that *everyone* can follow. Literally everyone. People with mental illness. People in poverty. People with special needs. Even the young people who live with us that we call "our children." Because if they've got no place in our vision of the successful Christian life, whatever it is we're selling, it isn't a truly *Christian* life.

This is why we believe the best discipleship practices should begin in the easiest possible form—not because following Jesus is always easy (it isn't), but because we want everyone who follows Jesus—our neighbors and our friends and our littlest kids—to have a step they can actually take. We want people to know that *God wants to be with you.* And that means that following Jesus is, first and foremost, a matter of *being with Him.*

Wouldn't it be better for everyone in a church to take a few baby steps than for just one or two people to become super Christians?

MAKE A CLEAR AND EASY PATH

Change is tough. The Christian life, if practiced rightly, is tough. Which is precisely why we shouldn't make it *even tougher*. We've got to start with something easy.

When it comes to starting a spiritual habit, here's what we've learned: *Make a clear and easy plan—something you can start in five minutes or less.*

Remember, when we're starting something new, we're fighting against the metaphorical "Steves" and "Kristens" in our head. Decision fatigue is pushing us toward autopilot, which makes any truly new decision tiring. So keep it simple and keep it small.

For instance, most of us want to pray more often. But when the moment comes, we're presented with a dozen decisions: *Where will I sit? Wait, should I kneel? Should I begin with the Lord's Prayer? Or some other prayer? Do I even know another prayer by heart? Weren't there people I said I'd pray for? Should I read my Bible as part of this? How long am I supposed to do this?* It's a lot.

In contrast, the sight of your phone—which is most likely within arm's reach—easily reminds you that you *could* be playing the Chess app instead. You've done it every night for the past week anyway. You know just how to do it. Honestly, it doesn't even feel like a decision. Autopilot.

Checkmate.

Rather than berating yourself for being a bad Christian, we believe it's possible to change some of the circumstances to make the right choice just a bit easier. It will still take some work. But decision fatigue doesn't have to win.

Make a clear and easy plan—something you can start in five minutes or less.

Let's break that down into three parts: (1) Forgive yourself, (2) Make it easier than (you think) you have to, and (3) Write it down.

YOUR FIRST THREE STEPS

1. Forgive Yourself

Picture this scene: You're scrolling through Instagram when you see Influencer Jessica talk about her prayer life. This seems promising enough, so you pause the scroll to hear her out.

Apparently Jessica has revolutionized her prayer life. She feels closer to God now than ever before. All it took was praying this specific way—which she didn't know about until she read some very cool-sounding author you've never heard of. Jessica promises to share this revolutionary way of life with you, too. You can read more about it on her blog. Or you can pick up her book. Or you can join her at the retreat center she hosts on her family's farm.

By the end of the reel, you're rolling your eyes. *This isn't anything like my life,* you think, *and there's no way I can ever get there.*

Maybe it's not Jessica, but it's your pastor. During a three-week sermon series on prayer, he mentions his own prayer habit—setting aside time every morning, for an hour, to pray before he does any other work.

You're encouraged that your pastor is praying. But you can't relate. Your day starts when your three-year-old jumps into your bed at six thirty a.m. And you aren't in ministry, so the prospect of showing up to the office, then disappearing to pray for an hour . . . doesn't seem viable.

We can give your pastor and Influencer Jessica the benefit of the doubt here. They really may have found a good rhythm for prayer in their own lives. The trouble comes when we take *their* reality and make it *our* target. But we aren't living someone else's life. We're living our own. God doesn't expect us to match someone else. He expects us to faithfully follow him.

Which means we need to forgive ourselves for not measuring up to everyone else's standards.

Someone in ministry will have more flexibility to add prayer to their work day than someone who isn't. Parents of a newborn will have less mental energy than young couples without kids. Your life situation is unique, and while it shifts from season to season, it always makes a huge difference. (As dads of elementary-aged kids, we speak from experience!)

So forgive yourself. Remember, *God is gracious.*

There are dozens of ways to pray. For instance, you can pray through the Lord's Prayer. Or you can follow the acrostic "ACTS," which stands for Adoration, Confession, Thanksgiving, Supplication. You can read a psalm and then respond to God. You can read scripted prayers from church history. You can keep a prayer journal of all the people you're praying for.

Here's what you *can't* do—all of that, every time you pray. You just can't.

As we were working on this book, Clayton asked me, "What's the best type of prayer?" My answer: It's the one you are doing.

Forgive yourself for what you're not doing and build on what you are doing.

Celebrate What Is Already Working

Throughout this book, we are pausing from time to time to help you celebrate what is already working. When it comes to spiritual habits, chances are you're already getting a lot of things right. Yes, you.

The point of this book isn't just to offer you new tools, but also to help you recognize and celebrate the bright spots that are already there. We've found that just giving these bright spots their time to shine allows them to shine all the brighter.

Many of us are quick to explain away good spiritual habits because we have some internal vision of what *real* spiritual habits might look like. (And we, somehow, aren't measuring up to it.) But don't skip what's already working in your life. Instead, look for the moments where you already do give attention to God and to others. Then celebrate those moments.

Rather than assessing your spiritual life by looking for all the parts that are broken, ask yourself what's going well. Is there an aspect of your spiritual life, right now, that is healthy and good? For instance, do you go to church on a regular basis? Do you have a spiritual podcast you listen to? Do you attend a church small group or Bible study? Do you listen to worship music? Do you pray at night with your kids? (Yes, that counts.) Are you reading a book about spiritual life? (Yes, *this* one counts!)

Take an inventory right now: Give your rhythms a decent audit, and don't be afraid to call some of them *good*.

2. Make It Easier than You Think You Have To

Our friend Philip struggled to make working out a priority—until one day, he tried a new approach. Rather than setting a goal of running twenty miles a week or lifting five times a week, he set an absurdly easy new goal: *Drive to the gym parking lot three times a week.* He didn't even have to go *into* the gym. To get credit, he just had to drive there. And some days, he would do exactly that. He drove to the gym, circled the parking lot, and then went right back home. But most days, having gotten to the gym, he figured, *Well, I'm already here. Might as well do a little something.*

Philip made his fitness goal tremendously easy—far easier than he thought he had to. But he met his goal. And it gave him positive momentum, so that he didn't wash out after two weeks.

Another friend of ours, Anna, was tired of harassing her kids to clean up their rooms. So she started a new cleanup game. She plays one song that the kids like (usually Taylor Swift), and the kids have to clean up for the length of the song. Once the song is over, their responsibility is finished. If the room is half clean, that's fine. But often, once they get going, the kids decide it's easier to just finish the job.

The goal here—whether we're talking about cleaning up or working out or reading your Bible—isn't to stay at that lowest level. Obviously, we want to do *more* than our stated goal. But when we're doing something new, we have to do our minds a favor and keep it small. Otherwise we get excited at the beginning, sprinting out far faster than we can maintain. And our excited beginning only lasts a few days.

To counteract this, we need to make our habits easier than we think we have to. In *Atomic Habits*, James Clear puts it like this: "The idea is to make it as easy as possible in the moment to do things that pay off in the long run."[6] If all Philip is doing for his workout routine, three years from now, is driving to the gym repeatedly, we'd all say he's missed the mark. But with a super easy goal *today*, he's more likely to be working out in three years. Which is, in the end, what he was going for all along.

To help kick-start easy habits, experts often suggest time limits—and incredibly short ones. James Clear calls it "the two-minute rule."[7] Doing two minutes of anything seems doable, right? And then, with repetition, two-minute habits tend to grow.

So instead of "Walk more often," you might say, "Take one lap around the building during my lunch break."

Instead of "Read more books," or even "Read fifty books this year," you might say, "Read for two minutes each morning before I get out of bed."

What's true for exercise or reading is true for spiritual habits, too. Rather than aiming to pray for ten minutes a day, you could make your goal to kneel twice a day. Rather than reading the Bible in a year, you could make your goal to read a chapter a day. Rather than turning your phone off for twenty-four hours for the Sabbath, you start by turning it off for thirty minutes.

Following Jesus is a habit that should become a lifestyle. Because *God works slowly* and *God is gracious*, the steps are small and the pace is slow. But that's how God does His best work in us—slower than we might like, but more sure than we can imagine.

3. Write It Down

Once you've made your habit easy—even easier than you thought you needed to—it's time to write it down. Writing it down helps you remember your goal. (As we've heard it said, "The dullest pencil is sharper than the brightest mind.") Writing it down gives you more ownership, helps you overcome decision paralysis, and makes it easier to share your goals with others, which is something we'll discuss in chapter 8.

So why don't you do that now? Go back to the spiritual habit you chose at the end of the last chapter. Now, jot down your "easier than you think" goal with that habit. Make sure it's easier than you think it needs to be, ideally something you can start in less than five minutes. If it seems too easy—and feels even embarrassingly easy—then you're on the right track:

I will _____.

You probably wrote your answer in pen, which is fine. But just know that, metaphorically, this goal is going to stay in pencil for now. Because over the course of the rest of this book, we're going to keep coming back to that habit, editing, tinkering, practicing, starting, and starting *over*.

Don't worry about the fact that this goal will change. For now, what we want is to make it **easy** and **clear**. Remember, like the Heath brothers mentioned, "What looks like resistance is often a lack of clarity." At this point, we simply need something concrete to work with.

Have you got your **one spiritual habit** in mind and **one goal** to go along with it? Great! That may seem like a small step, but it's an important one. As Mary Poppins once quipped, "Well begun is half done."[8]

Now, let's keep going!

SMALL STEPS YOU CAN TAKE TODAY

At the end of each chapter in Part Two, we've provided a section called "Small Steps You Can Take Today," where we offer a few super practical (and super small) applications. For each chapter, we'll focus on just *one* spiritual habit, highlighting just *one* small step you can make. You don't have to do all of them—in fact, you shouldn't. Pick up one or two of the ideas that seem like they'd work for you. Such as . . .

Sabbath: Sabbath is a habit of enjoying what God has given us.

We begin with Sabbath because we all need it, we've all heard about it, but very few of us actually do it. What are some small steps you can take toward Sabbath today? Here are a couple of ideas:

Building a Sabbath habit in the home—for families
- Make It Easy: Just plan a fun, weekly kickoff meal and call it a Sabbath Meal.

Building a Sabbath habit in the home—for grown-ups
- Make It Easy: Okay, taking a break from our phone is hard, but it's good for us. Don't go cold turkey, attempting twenty-four straight hours without your phone. Instead, find a key moment in your weekly rhythms that already breaks the cycle of work. Decide to kick-start a break from your phone in under five minutes. Just do something to appreciate the week and celebrate God's gifts to you. Then, make sure to use the word *Sabbath*.

Make It Tangible

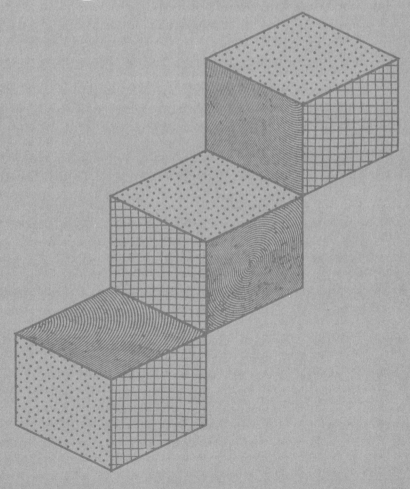

CHAPTER FOUR

Question: Do you have something physical that reminds you of the spiritual habit?

Our "small step" suggestion: Have a tangible strategy for cueing your attention to the spiritual aspects of life.

Set a cue that:

- . . . you can touch.
- . . . you trip over.
- . . . distracts you from your phone.
- . . . works for you, not for us.

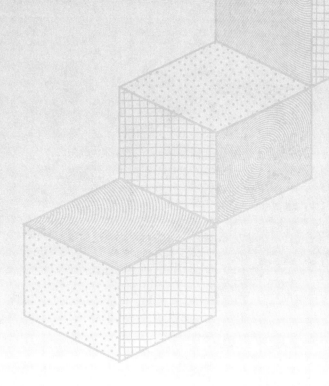

Hey, Look, a Bear!

Have you ever seen one of those tricky "awareness test" videos?[1] The one Clayton made me watch recently began with two teams of people holding basketballs—one team wearing black and the other wearing white. The voiceover said, "Count all the passes the white team makes." So I watched, doing my best to pay attention, as they danced around and tossed the balls back and forth. *One, two, three . . .* By the time it finished and the voiceover announced, "The answer was thirteen!" I felt pretty proud of myself. *I had gotten it right! Mark an "A" on my awareness test!*

Then the voiceover announced, "But did you notice the moonwalking bear?" Wait . . . *what?*

Sure enough, the same video played again, and *are you kidding me*, there was a person dressed as a bear who moonwalked right across the screen. Slowly. But I was so focused on counting passes that the bear literally didn't register.

Like I said, tricky.

The point of the video isn't to make viewers feel like dummies. (Okay, the *main* point isn't to make viewers feel like dummies.) The video is meant to highlight an important truth: You rarely notice something you aren't looking for.

Paying attention to what matters is hard work. But paying attention seems harder today than it has ever been. Notifications tug at your shirt sleeves to *check your email, read this clickbaity article, answer that Slack message, respond to those Instagram comments, act on this once-in-a-lifetime, 75-percent-off sale!* Not only is this World of Notifications exhausting, but it torpedoes our capacity to pay attention.

Here's what makes that a spiritual problem: God is active every day, in a thousand different ways, all around us. But He doesn't come at us like the freight train of iPhone notifications. He nudges. He guides. He whispers in silent, still moments. Which means if we don't have the capacity to pay attention, we're likely to miss Him.

As John Mark Comer put it, many of us complain that God feels absent. But in the twenty-first century, it's much more likely that we are the ones who are absent.[2]

Most of us don't need to be convinced of this. We've heard the studies about our attention spans having become worse than that of goldfish. We've read the headlines about social media rotting our brains. We get it already—we are distracted people.

We know attention is difficult. What we don't know is, *How can we grasp our own attention?*

Or, to put it a bit differently, *How do we pay attention to God?*

SPIRITUAL SPEED BUMPS

To make spiritual habits stick, we need habits that help us pay attention—to God, to others, to our own thoughts and feelings. Habits that bring us out of the autopilot of our day so we can notice what God may be doing around us. We need spiritual speed bumps.

Why do literal, physical speed bumps exist? To slow you down, right? Sorta. Yes, the speed bump is supposed to slow you down. But ultimately, the slowing isn't the point. The point is (usually), *there are people walking around here.* We slow down because we're moving two tons of metal through a parking lot and we need to pay attention to pedestrians.

Spiritual speed bumps—Sabbath, prayer, silence—serve a similar function. They slow us down, yes (which is why John Mark Comer calls "slowing," in itself, a spiritual discipline).[3] But the slowing isn't the ultimate goal. The slowing is the means; paying attention to the spiritual is the end. Slowing allows us to pay attention to what matters. It leaves space for us to notice what only the Holy Spirit can do—speak, guide, confront, heal.

Our world moves *fast*. Often that's wonderful and exciting. (Thank God for wireless internet. Dial-up was rough.) But as much as we've grown used to rushing through life, we've got to admit that moving fast isn't turning us into the people we want to be. If we want to become people of patience, hope, and gratitude, it won't happen in the frantic moments. It happens in the slower ones. After all, that's the pace God prefers to work. He transforms us as we crawl over the spiritual speed bumps.

The good news is, no matter how fast we're flying, we can learn to slow down. We can pause long enough to ask, "How has God been good to me today?" We can begin to notice the everyday moments that have the potential to surprise us, delight us, or provoke some new insight.

Author Matthew Sleeth once said, "The world isn't in need of more *wonders*. It's in need of more *wonder-ment*."[4] Our task isn't to seek out new wonders. It's to slow down and ask God to show us the wonders He has already provided.

But we're at an impasse again. We *know* we're supposed to slow down. We *know* we need spiritual speed bumps. But what do they look like?

Our answer: It looks like something you can touch. Physical, tactile . . . tangible.

Just like God had always intended.

ALTARS AND BREAD AND OUR TANGIBLE GOD

Knowing our tendency to be easily distracted, God made worship tangible. The word "tangible" literally means "perceptible by touch." This probably isn't the first word that comes to mind when we think of God—and for good reason. In the Old Testament laws, God made a big deal out of not making physical representations of Him. It was one of God's top ten rules, the second of the Ten Commandments (Ex. 20:4–6). Jesus Himself said, "God is spirit," which feels like the opposite of tangible (John 4:24). And the writer of Hebrews summarized the Christian life by saying, "Faith is the assurance of things hoped for, the conviction of things not seen" (Heb. 11:1).

It seems to be in the very nature of God that He cannot be contained or controlled. As we mentioned in chapter 1, *we can't see God.* And if we can't see Him, we certainly can't hold Him or touch Him. We can't wrap our minds around God, let alone our feeble fingers.

But this is one of the surprises of Scripture: The God who *should* be beyond our reach consistently makes our spiritual habits tangible. God Himself may be an intangible Spirit, but He knows how thoroughly tangible we are. So for as long as God has invited people to worship Him, He has done so in thoroughly tangible ways.

In the Old Testament, for instance, one of the most consistent responses people have after meeting with God is to construct an altar. *God starts,* and the go-to response, as often as not, is, "I had better get building." Noah built an altar after God led him and his family through the flood (Gen. 8:20). Abraham built an altar after God first revealed Himself to him—then again when God spared his son, Isaac (Gen. 12:7; 22:9). Isaac himself built an altar after God's revelation to him (Gen. 26:25). The tradition continued to Abraham's grandson, Jacob, who built an altar to commemorate the place God met him as he fled his brother, Esau (Gen. 35:7).

Moses built an altar after a great military victory (Ex. 17:15). Moses' successor, Joshua, built an altar the moment God's people crossed into the promised land (Josh. 4:1–7). And on and on it goes—Gideon, Manoah (Samson's father), Samuel, Saul, David, Solomon, Elijah, Joshua and Zerubbabel—*all* of them built altars to God (Judg. 6:26–27; 13:19–20; 1 Sam. 7:17; 14:35; 2 Sam. 24:18–25; 1 Kings 6:20–21; 18:30–39; Ezra 3:2–3).

Why altars? Practically, the altar served an immediate and pragmatic purpose: It was a location for a burnt offering. If you were going to roast an animal to sacrifice to God (and the sacrificial system was *huge* in the Old Testament), you needed a place to cook it.

But altars were much more than pragmatic spots for a religious barbecue. Just as importantly, they acted as tangible prompts for future generations. As Joshua said about his altar, "These stones shall be to the people of Israel a memorial forever" (Josh. 4:7). Altars were a tangible reminder of an intangible God, a physical reminder that although they couldn't see God, *He was there*.

Even when God's people weren't building altars, God made certain that their worship would be tangible. For proof of this, look to the most prominent event of the Old Testament—God rescuing His people from bondage in Egypt. God's people commemorated this saving moment with an annual ritual called Passover, named for God "passing over" the homes of the Israelites but visiting the homes of the oppressive Egyptians with death.

The Passover tradition was predominantly a shared meal. During Passover, families gathered to enjoy lamb, unleavened bread, wine, and a collection of herbs. The meal intentionally mirrored the meal God's people shared on the night before their rescue: Lambs were slaughtered to provide blood for the doorposts; the bread was unleavened because the exodus would happen in a hurry.

And what was the purpose of the Passover meal? This is how Moses put it:

"This day shall be for you a memorial day, and you shall keep it as a feast to the LORD; throughout your generations, as a statute forever, you shall keep it as a feast.... And it shall be to you as a sign on your hand and as a memorial between your eyes, that the law of the LORD may be in your mouth. For with a strong hand the LORD has brought you out of Egypt." (Ex. 12:14; 13:9)

In a word, *remember*. God gave His people a meal so they would remember their rescue. With every bite of bread and lamb, with every sip of wine, God's people could taste His goodness.

There are other beautiful and essential elements to Passover—for instance, recounting the exodus story. But at the center sits a meal. God didn't just tell His people to share His stories. Instead, He created a spiritual rhythm that people could touch and taste—eat this bread; eat this lamb.

It's fair to say that very few, if any, of the Old Testament people of God anticipated what God would do next. They may have known that God made worship tangible. But they couldn't have guessed that God would go a step further—not merely making worship tangible, but making *Himself* tangible. And yet, in Jesus, that's precisely what happened.

The incarnation—that is, the doctrine of God becoming human in Jesus—still stuns me. Perhaps it shouldn't. Because it has *always* been stunning to believe that God was intimately involved in our little, physical, tangible world. And yet, He always has been. The altars and Passover meals were always meant to remind God's people that He was near, active, involved. And in the end, they all pointed to Jesus, God in the flesh. A tangible person, just like you and me.

During His final meal with the disciples, Jesus picked up the bread and wine of Passover and transformed the tradition forever. His disciples were used to seeing the bread and wine as tangible reminders of God's saving power. But that saving power was all in the past, limited to their ancestors in Egypt. Jesus still wanted them to remember, but during His last meal, He filled the ancient practice with new meaning.

No longer would the bread remind His people of their ancestors' quick exit from Egypt. Instead, it would remind the disciples of Jesus' sacrificial death. Jesus, the Lamb of God, was about to be sacrificed to free His people from slavery—not slavery to Egypt, but slavery to sin and death. *Remember this*, Jesus said.

No longer would the wine remind His people of the covenant God made with their ancestors. Instead, it would remind the disciples of Jesus' new covenant, one sealed with His blood and open to people of every tribe, tongue, and nation. *Remember this and remember me,* Jesus said.

The meaning of the meal had changed forever. But at no point did Jesus make it *less* tangible. To the very end, He kept the practice tangible: Keep eating this bread, keep drinking this wine. And the reasoning was the same, too: *By sharing this meal, you will remember what I've done for you.*

Jesus knew that we flesh-and-blood creatures would need tangible reminders of truth. So instead of a speech on salvation, He said, "Eat, drink, and remember."

REMINDER-ING LEADS TO REMEMBERING

What is it that makes tangible reminders so effective? It's the difference between *remembering* something important and being *reminded* of something important.

For instance, if we told you to *remember* to send our friend Brian a birthday card on October 20 this year—without writing anything down or creating a reminder of any sort—how likely is it that you would do it?

About as likely as you having sent him a card last year. Which is to say, 0.0 percent. It just won't happen.

Is the problem that you don't value Brian? Doubtful. Even if you were friends with him (and he's great, you'd love him), you probably wouldn't have his birthday memorized. If it mattered to you, *you'd write it down somewhere.* Because you intuitively know: Remembering is harder than reminder-ing. Now just imagine that you can't even see Brian. Gets even tougher, doesn't it? Remember, *we can't see God, but He is there.*

Some of us might think that setting reminders feels a bit like cheating—as if the only way a spiritual habit "counts" is if we do it without prompting. But that's not how we operate in other important parts of our lives. And it's not an expectation we get from Scripture, either. God has always given His people reminders, specifically to *help* them in their remembering.

Consider, for instance, the words of the apostle Peter:

Therefore I intend always *to remind* you of these qualities, though you know them and are established in the truth that you have. I think it right, as long as I am in this body, to stir you up by way of *reminder,* since I know that the putting off of my body will be soon, as our Lord Jesus Christ made clear to me. And I will make every effort so that after my departure you may be able at any time *to recall* these things. (2 Peter 1:12–15, emphasis added[5])

Do you see the connection Peter makes? He is writing, *as a reminder,* so that people will "be able at any time to recall" the truths he's sharing. In other words, the reminder-ing leads to the remembering.

We've all experienced this in other areas of our lives, right? The authors of the book *Influencer* give a classic example: Imagine your neighbor has just survived a heart attack. The doctor's orders are clear. He needs to drastically alter his diet. Less red meat, fewer sweets.

This is the best way to stay healthy and survive long enough to see his grandkids. But the next time you get dinner with your neighbor, he decides to order the biggest dessert on the menu.

What is happening at that moment? Has your neighbor decided that he doesn't care about seeing his grandchildren? Probably not. It's more likely that he's simply not thinking of them. He's not connecting the dots between his dietary decisions and his future relationships.[6]

What matters in these situations is not how much you care (this is what we often assume) but what you are thinking about (this is what we often miss). The trouble isn't necessarily a moral failure. It's a matter of attention. Your neighbor is distracted from what he *ought* to be thinking about. Given the right reminder, he greatly improves his odds of making better dietary choices.

So give yourself some grace. You wanted to pray for your friend, but you slept in instead. You wanted to read your Bible before bed, but you got sucked into an hour of scrolling Instagram instead.

When that happens, don't conclude you're a spiritual failure. After all, remembering is hard.

Hard, but not impossible. Because you can *remind* yourself.

HOW TO BUILD YOUR SPIRITUAL SPEED BUMPS

Speaking of reminders, here's an important one: Don't forget that you're just focusing on *one* spiritual habit for now. We're not trying to build spiritual speed bumps for all of life—not yet, anyway. One at a time.

With that one spiritual habit, you've already done some work in the last chapter to make the plan as easy as possible. Now you need to set tangible cues that remind you to kick-start that easy plan.

So, the question becomes, *How can you create these tangible reminders for yourself?*

What would it look like for you to build "spiritual speed bumps" that slow you down long enough to make a spiritual habit more likely?

1. Set a Cue That You Can Touch

If there's one thing you take away from this chapter, it ought to be: The best spiritual speed bumps are physical and tangible. You've got to be able to pick them up.

Don't just take our word for it. In *Atomic Habits*, James Clear mentions several examples of helpful cues. Look what they all have in common:

- To remember to take your meds, "put your pill bottle ... on the bathroom sink."
- To practice guitar more often, "place the guitar in the middle of the living room."
- To send more thank-you notes, "keep a stack of stationery on your desk."[7]

What all of these examples have in common is the physical nature of the cue. In theory, a phone reminder would accomplish the same task. But we're all so used to dismissing notifications on our phone that we'd likely ignore that one, too. On the other hand, a physical object, something you can touch, is much tougher to ignore.

For a spiritual habit, this might mean that you:

- Leave a stack of Bible memory verses in a high traffic area, like your front door or in your car.
- Place a prayer jar in the kitchen and write requests on popsicle sticks.
- Stash your phone *under* your journal, so you have to physically pick up your journal *first*—even if only to move it out of the way.

2. Set a Cue That You Trip Over

No, not literally. We're talking about attention here, not your feet. Choosing the right object is a good start. But it's got to be something that captures your attention, too. The most powerful discipleship resource in the world won't do you a lick of good if you pass by it a hundred times without ever wanting to pick it up.

In *The Tech-Wise Family*, Andy Crouch mentions the "nudge power" of everyday objects: "I want a life of conversation and friendship, not distraction and entertainment; but every day, many times a day, I'm *nudged* in the wrong direction. One key part of the art of living faithfully with technology is setting up better *nudges* for ourselves."[8]

Many of the objects in our homes create *nudges* toward different kinds of behavior. Some objects—for instance, a television—nearly demand that you stop and engage. Others invite you in more subtly—for instance, a piano. And some—like an electric socket—don't exercise much nudge power at all (unless you're two years old, of course).

It's important that we take stock of what actually captures our attention and what blends into the background. Not all that surrounds us nudges us with equal force. Some objects nudge us more than others, and the placement is often the reason why. (We'll get more into that in the next chapter, actually.) A Christian quote or a Bible verse on the wall may be beautiful and meaningful, but in our experience, it tends to become decor. And decor doesn't act as a spiritual speed bump. It doesn't nudge us. Instead, it becomes part of your background.

Your tangible cue has to be a little bit intrusive. Not iPhone-notification intrusive, exactly, but certainly not blends-into-the-background decor, either.

We recently saw this in action while working on a product we call "Sticky Prayers." They are stickers you can put on your phone, water bottle, computer—anywhere you want to be reminded to pause and pray. The first batch we got were beautiful, which was a win. But the texture was so thin they were easy to ignore. So we made the next batch much bumpier. That little change helped us "trip over" the object much more, giving us the chance to pause and pray.

Celebrate What Is Already Working

Let's take this one to the most basic level imaginable: Do you ever eat food or sleep?

Eating and sleeping, two of the most fundamental experiences, are also speed bumps in our daily lives. They slow us down. And whether we savor the slowing or resent it, we simply can't avoid it. Our bodies need food. They need rest. They need to slow down and stop pretty often.

So own the goodness of these pause points. Maybe you don't sit down to eat leisurely meals every day. (Breakfast in the car, anyone?) But I'm guessing you have some meals that are slower. Celebrate that as a tangible and tasty speed bump, slowing you down to focus on what's right in front of you.

And each night, as you lie down to sleep, recognize that your bed is a tangible reminder of your limits. Accept those limits as God's gift to you. And get cozy.

You don't necessarily need to add prayer to each of these pause points—though it couldn't hurt. For now, just recognize the speed bumps in your life and accept them as God's interrupting grace.

3. Set a Cue That Distracts You from Your Phone

I'm sure this isn't a huge surprise to you. In the battle for our attention, the smartphone often acts like a supervillain. Whether you love your phone or hate it, you have to recognize that it has made it much more difficult to be present and attentive.

We're not about to solve the problem of tech addiction in four brisk paragraphs. Fortunately, many other great writers have offered a ton of wisdom here, and we'd encourage you to pick up one of their books.[9] Our point here is simply to encourage you to find a physical object that can outdo your phone in what your phone does best—capture your attention.

Have you ever gotten caught up in a beautiful moment and lost track of time? The moment doesn't have to be grand to be engrossing. Maybe you were playing *Throw Throw Burrito* with your kids. Or reading a really great book. Or listening to music while you cooked dinner. Or laughing with your friends around a campfire. Seriously, think about the last time this happened to you. What were you doing? Where were you? Who was there?

Where was your phone?

I'm willing to bet that the last time you lost yourself in some activity you loved, some physical object—or some physical environment—played a central role. (This is worlds away from the icky feeling of having an hour disappear while we're scrolling Instagram.) Granted, you can't always manufacture moments of delight. But these moments provide a clue for overcoming our phone dependence. Dig into them and see if any physical objects stand out.

4. Set a Cue That Works for You, Not for Us

We've offered a lot of examples in this chapter. Some of them will work wonders for you. Others won't. Effective cues are usually individually tailored. So find the ones that work for you, not the ones that have worked for us.

And don't be afraid to engage in some trial and error. We've tried out *dozens* of cues we thought sounded fantastic, only to find that they didn't quite take. That's the process.

With a little intentionality and creativity, you can create spiritual speed bumps in your living room, your bedroom, your office, your car, or anywhere else.

From there, who knows what the Spirit will do next?

SMALL STEPS YOU CAN TAKE TODAY

Prayer: A conversation God has started with us and we continue in many ways.

Prayer can be lament, praise, thanksgiving, silence. The possibilities are nearly endless, which can be overwhelming. What are some small steps you can take toward prayer today? Here are a few ideas:

Building a prayer habit in the home—for families

- Make It Easy: Pray for one thing—just one thing—at bedtime. Literally make it a one sentence start.
- **Make It Tangible: Use popsicle sticks in a jar to rotate through all the requests your little one wants to pray about. Pick one at night, and put it back in upside down when you are done. Repeat. Keep a few blank popsicle sticks and a pen close by.**

Building a prayer habit in the home—for grown-ups

- Make It Easy: Decide to kneel for thirty seconds in the morning before your day begins.
- **Make It Tangible: A kneeling pad is a great tangible item to use for prayer. You can put it by a bed, a dresser, a desk. If the goal is to get into the posture, this cue is excellent and helps you actually build the habit.**

Pick a Place

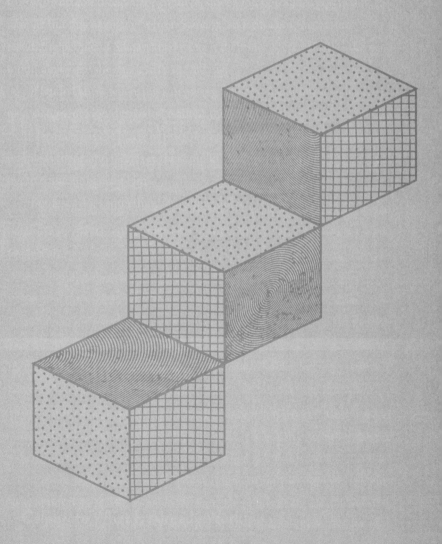

CHAPTER FIVE

Question: Do you have a specific place where you do this spiritual habit?

Our "small step" suggestion: Think as much about *where* you do spiritual habits as you think about *what* spiritual habits you are going to do.

1. **Where is the room?** Pick a convenient place you pass often.

2. **What does the room feel like?** Pick a place that is inviting and free of distractions.

3. **What is in the room?** Pick a place that has items conducive to the spiritual habit.

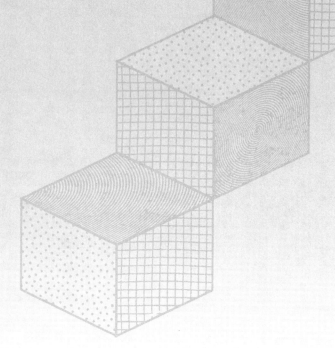

Surrounded by Books and Ready to Go

A good friend of ours—we'll call him Michael—loves to visit bookstores and libraries. Michael is, unsurprisingly, an avid reader. But his love for the bookstore isn't primarily about the books. It's about what happens *in him* when he enters the bookstore.

And by "in him," we mean literally—inside of his body. Because like clockwork, within five minutes of stepping into a bookstore, Michael's body tells him that it's time to use the bathroom. (Yes, we're talking about number two here. No, we won't get any more graphic than that.)

Michael's theory is that, being a book lover, the presence of books is so calming that it allows his body to relax. And when your body relaxes, it's much easier to . . . go.

For years, Michael thought he was the only one. We did, too. Then we looked it up online. And it turns out, there are countless "Michaels" out there for whom the bookstore or library—or even the book section of Target—gets the process swiftly sailing along. Scientifically, it's still not entirely clear *why* this happens.[1] But for many people, there's definitely a connection.

If you're one of those people, like Michael, who holds a special place in your heart for the magical gastrointestinal power of the bookstore, we hope you feel a little less alone. If you can't relate at all (and find all of this bizarre and a little gross), take heart—we're finished with the illustration.

The environment around us matters. And as Michael's story reminds us, that environment often works on us in subtle, subconscious ways.

Have you ever walked into a room and immediately *felt* something? Maybe it was some unspoken tension among everyone gathered there. Maybe it was a calming sense of welcome. Maybe it was a wave of awe. Whatever you felt, you didn't get that feeling by rationally making a choice. *Oh, I'm looking at stained glass windows. I'll decide to feel reverent now.* No, the environment did its work on *all* of your senses, and your mind was the last to catch up.

Whether we realize it or not, the environment around us matters. But what if, rather than merely being affected by the environments around us, we intentionally shaped our environments, instead? As James Clear puts it in *Atomic Habits*, "You don't have to be the victim of your environment. You can also be the architect of it."[2]

A few changes to the environment around you can mean the difference between feeling calm and feeling agitated. Or, since we're talking spiritual habits here, the difference between a pattern of prayer and a lifestyle of prayerlessness.

FROM HEAVEN TO A BURNING MOUNTAIN

Here's a theological statement you've probably never heard before: God has always been keenly concerned with *His* physical environment.

Again, as an example, let's go back to the pinnacle Old Testament story of God's saving power—the exodus from Egypt. For centuries, God's people had suffered as slaves under an oppressive king. They were numerous, but they were powerless. All of that changed, nearly overnight, when God brought His power against the power of Egypt. It took ten miraculous plagues to break the will of the Egyptian king. But eventually, God's power triumphed—and hundreds of thousands of His people walked out of Egypt, finally free.

As they marched away from their oppressors, they saw God's presence in a frightening display—a pillar of cloud by day and a pillar of fire by night. The same power that had turned the Nile to blood and blotted out the sun was now visible in front of them, leading them into the wilderness.

The people watched, in awe, as the pillar of fire climbed up Mount Sinai, making the entire mountain shake and sputter like a volcano. God was present on that mountain, and His presence was terrifying.

"You shall set limits for the people," God said, "all around [the mountain], saying, 'Take care not to go up into the mountain or touch the edge of it. Whoever touches the mountain shall be put to death'" (Ex. 19:12). The people got the message: God's presence isn't something warm and fuzzy. It's awe-inspiring, even frightening.

It's important to keep in mind that the power wasn't in this specific location. This mountain didn't add a thing to who God was—but it was an unmistakable physical representation of who He was.

You might think God displayed all of this volcanic fury to keep people away from Him. Not exactly. God actually wanted to invite His people closer to Him. Even in this frightening moment, *God wanted to be with His people.* He wanted to draw them close, giving them words of freedom and life. But He also knew they needed to be prepared to receive those words.

In fact, as Exodus 20 shows us, in the end, it wasn't God who pushed the people back, but the other way around: "Now when all the people saw the thunder and the flashes of lightning and the sound of the trumpet and the mountain smoking, the people were afraid and trembled, and they stood far off and said to Moses, 'You speak to us, and we will listen; but do not let God speak to us, lest we die'" (Ex. 20:18–19). Fear and trembling was exactly the right response. They needed to remember just how *great* this God was. But the next step they took—telling Moses to do business with God on their behalf—was a tragic one. They missed out on the opportunity to hear, firsthand, just how *good* this God was. They missed the invitation God had for them: *Come and be with me.*

So only Moses got to sit with God in the environment He had prepared.

FROM A BURNING MOUNTAIN TO A BEAUTIFUL TEMPLE

From Sinai onward, God continued to choose specific locations to be His designated resting places. At first it was the mountain. But it soon shifted: Moses actually came down from Mount Sinai with God's plan to place His presence in a tent, called the tabernacle. *God still wanted to be with His people,* and this was the new method.

For centuries, the tabernacle was *the* place God's presence could be found. Elaborate regulations protected who was allowed into this holy place, and how. Tabernacle priests had to have the right wardrobe, the right tools, the right sacrifices—and above all, a holy life. Just as it had been on Mount Sinai, it was a fearful thing to enter into God's presence, not to be taken lightly.

But distinct from God's Sinai environment, the tabernacle was also a place of tremendous beauty. The priestly garments were adorned with precious stones. The curtains within the tabernacle were dyed in vibrant purples, blues, and reds. There was fragrant incense and expensive oils for the lamps. And there was gold *all* over the place.

For example, when the tabernacle transitioned from a traveling tent to a permanent temple, King Solomon collected 1,086 talents (roughly 34 tons) of gold. To put that number in context, that amount of gold would cost about $1.9 billion today.[3] And there was far less refined gold in the world then, too; some scholars estimate that Solomon's offering amounted to *half* the gold supply in the ancient world.[4]

In the tabernacle—and later, the temple—God's fearful presence was also a beautiful presence. And God's people knew this, in part, because of the environment He built for Himself.

They also knew how limited God's earthly presence was—in this one place, in this one city, among this one people.

If you were an Old Testament believer, you could measure your closeness to God with literal geographic precision. That's not to say that you could measure *holiness* based on location. But God had chosen to place His presence in a very specific environment.

In a sense, the farther you were from that special place, the farther you were from God. There was a simplicity to this, but also a profound difficulty: How could the whole world worship God if He only stayed in one place?

How could God be with you and me if we never made our way to His temple?

NO MORE MOUNTAINS, NO MORE TEMPLES

This was the difficulty lurking in the background of one of Jesus' more famous conversations, recorded in John 4. Traveling through Samaria, Jesus stopped at a well and struck up a conversation with a woman drawing water there. Not being particularly keen on where the conversation was going, the woman tried to end it by raising a theological quarrel:

> The woman said to him, "Sir, I perceive that you are a prophet. Our fathers worshiped on this mountain, but you say that in Jerusalem is the place where people ought to worship." (John 4:19–20)

The temple was in Jerusalem. There was good reason to conclude that true worship could only happen there, since God's presence was tied to the temple. But this woman was from Samaria, so Jerusalem was off-limits. As a result, the people of Samaria had chosen their *own* sacred place—the very mountain where she and Jesus were talking.

If I didn't know where this story was going next, I would guess that Jesus' next statement would have to be about the temple. Something like, "You're right, Jerusalem is the place for worship. You've read enough to know that the temple is there, and God is in the temple!" Maybe Jesus would have invited her to come along with Him.

But Jesus does something altogether different:

Jesus said to her, "Woman, believe me, the hour is coming when neither on this mountain nor in Jerusalem will you worship the Father. You worship what you do not know; we worship what we know, for salvation is from the Jews. But the hour is coming, and is now here, when the true worshipers will worship the Father in spirit and truth, for the Father is seeking such people to worship him. God is spirit, and those who worship him must worship in spirit and truth." (John 4:21–24)

Wait a minute. *Not* in Jerusalem? What Old Testament was this guy reading?

The key lies in Jesus' reasoning: "God is spirit, and those who worship him must worship in spirit and truth" (John 4:24). What had made the temple sacred wasn't a specific place, but the Spirit of God that dwelled there. The same was true for the tabernacle before it, and the mountain before that. And the man standing there, taking His time to chat with this anonymous woman, carried within Him that very Spirit. He was the true temple, the embodiment of God on earth. Jesus was the living proof that *God wants to be with us.*

After His death and resurrection, Jesus would send that same Spirit into the hearts of every one of His followers (John 14:16, 26), forever breaking the categories of "holy place" and "unholy place."

This is as liberating for us as it was for the woman at the well. God's presence is not confined to a holy city, inaccessible to almost all of us. It's hard to overstate just how transformative this is. We don't need to go on a pilgrimage to get closer to the God of the universe. The fearful God of Sinai, the beautiful God of the temple: He's as close to me in my living room as He was to the woman at the well.

But as beautiful as this is, we have to recognize that it's also disorienting—because God is there, but we can't see Him. If all places can be holy (because of God's Spirit), what makes one place different from the next? I know I *can* commune with God just as well from Raleigh as Jerusalem, but I still feel the effects of different environments around me. And, if I do an honest audit, the environment around me rarely cultivates a sense of awe for God. In general, the environment I live in prompts me to buy more things and be more successful.

The physical presence of the temple said that God mattered *most*. Our environments, more often than not, don't communicate the same thing. They don't bring our attention to God at all. Remember, *God is there, but we can't see Him.* So we've still got some work to do.

Yes, it is better for us that all places can be places of worship. But it doesn't happen automatically. Remember James Clear's dichotomy: You can be the victim of your environment . . . or you can be the architect of your environment. The good news is, the difference between those two is often just a bit of intentionality.

WHAT THIS MEANS FOR SPIRITUAL HABITS: THREE QUESTIONS TO ANSWER

What does this look like when it comes to spiritual habits? Here are a few questions you need to answer, as noted at the beginning of this chapter: (1) Where is the room? (2) What does the room feel like? and (3) What is in the room?

1. Where Is the Room?

Technically, it doesn't have to be a room. It could be somewhere outside. It could even be your car. Wherever it is, your environment for your spiritual habits has to be **a convenient place you pass often**.

Let's bring this down to the mundane level again for a moment. People tend to go to the gym more if their gym is on the path of their normal drive to work. In offices, people tend to drink more coffee if their desk is closer to the coffee pot. In apartment complexes, close relationships are directly correlated to physical proximity, even if (in some other setting) people would have better chemistry with other neighbors.

Places you pass often become places that matter to you. Places off your beaten path don't seem to exist.

Clayton experienced this when he lived in Wilmington, North Carolina. The drive from his daughter's preschool to his office led him right by his gym. Sure enough, he ended up working out several times a week. But then his daughter changed preschools. The gym was still incredibly close—literally four minutes off of the route. But his workout routine took a nosedive. The gym wasn't a place he passed often. So it turned into a place he didn't go at all.

When choosing a place for your spiritual habits, lean toward places that are already close by. If it's a room in your house, don't make it the spare bedroom at the end of the upstairs hall; that's a cul-de-sac, not an intersection. Aim instead for the cozy chair in the corner of your bedroom. If it's some public space, don't choose a beautiful chapel forty-five minutes away from your office; aim instead for a quiet coffee shop you already know because it's on your commute.

For a season of my life, I got the chance to walk by a majestic church building every day—Duke University Chapel in Durham, North Carolina. The chapel is an awe-inspiring place, with beautiful stonework and elaborate stained glass windows that seem to extend endlessly upward. A giant organ fills the entire back wall, and when air flows through that organ, the reverent silence of the chapel suddenly transforms into transcendent music. You can feel it in your bones!

Duke Chapel was literally made for prayer. But what made the chapel a wonderful place for *me* to stop and pray was, more than anything, the location. I passed by it every day. It was already there. Today, even though I appreciate Duke Chapel far more than I ever did then, I haven't prayed in it for years. The reason is simple—it's a half-hour drive away. So for now, my living room chair is my holy place.

2. What Does the Room Feel Like?

A place for our spiritual habits should be **a place we *want* to be—inviting, soothing, calming**.

How many deep conversations have you had with someone in a grocery store? How about a coffee shop? Your back porch? At someone's bedside in the hospital?

Certain environments invite us to act in certain ways. Sure, it's possible to have rich, meaningful conversations in your local Harris Teeter. But the space isn't designed for that. The fluorescent lights buzz at you as you wander the aisles. The walls are packed with brightly colored items, each designed to draw your attention. Familiar pop music is constantly playing, periodically interrupted by ads (for the store you're already in).

I love my local Harris Teeter. But it's clearly a consumerist space, designed to get people moving and get people buying. It's not a space for lingering and connecting.

My local coffee shop, however (which you can see from Harris Teeter's automatic front doors), feels like a completely different world. The lighting is subdued. The walls are less packed, less loud, more likely to have paintings, plants, and books. Comfy chairs are everywhere. It's actually a bit louder than the grocery store, but it's the sound of connection—people sharing about their day, about their struggles.

When it comes to spiritual habits, far too many of us try to begin in environments more like the grocery store than the coffee shop. The spaces around us simply aren't designed to nudge us toward the habits we're after.

In her book *The Shaping of Us*, Lily Bernheimer refers to these as "behavior settings" (a phrase borrowed from 1950s psychologist Roger Barker). As she puts it,

> You may feel you act like yourself whether you're in a movie theatre or a post office. But Barker found that he could better predict a child's behaviour based on where he was than who he was. He called these "human-sized

units" of interaction "behaviour settings" . . . small social ecosystem[s], embedded in the bigger ecosystems of town, region, and country. Settings like candy shops, band practice, and X-ray laboratories, where people come to do certain activities at certain times in certain groups.[5]

Long before Bernheimer and Barker, God Himself made a unique "behavior setting"—the garden of Eden. Read through the first couple chapters of Genesis, the creation narrative, and notice what God chooses to mention (and what He doesn't). We'd like to know about literal timelines and scientific origins. Instead, God gives us line after line of poetry.

In the beginning, we are invited to watch the world's first days, painted with words, by God, the world's first artist.

Really, this shouldn't surprise us. Because what Genesis 1 describes is, itself, poetic and beautiful. Even before Adam and Eve arrive, the world is filled with diversity and delight. God prepares for them an extravagantly beautiful home.

We see a hint of that extravagance in Genesis 2:10–14, an otherwise odd passage about rivers and gemstone deposits. In this passage, the garden of Eden is given specific boundaries, some of which are known today. If we were to place Eden on a map, it wouldn't be like any tiny garden we've experienced. It would be more like Yellowstone National Park. Sprawling, enormous, rich, and wild.

And all of this for just two people. God was going *big* on beauty. Because God didn't just want a functional landing pad for Adam and Eve. God wanted an environment that felt as generous as He was.

Very few of us have the liberty to carve out our own garden of Eden. But we can do quite a bit to change the feel of a room. The most important thing is that a place for our spiritual habits should be a place we *want* to be—inviting, soothing, calming. It should be more like the coffee shop than the grocery store, more like a backyard firepit and less like a movie theater.

Celebrate What Is Already Working

We don't have a clue what your home looks like. But we do know this: It's designed to reflect your tastes. You decorated it with intentionality, even if—like us—there are still a dozen projects you'd like to get around to. You've already created your environment. Now you simply need to see what it is you've created.

So take a minute to walk through your home. What does each room feel like? Remember, you don't necessarily have to buy things or paint things to change how a room feels and flows.

One room in your home is already the most quiet. One room is the most conducive to community. One room is filled with technology. Notice what each room does to you as you enter it—and keep that in mind as you establish spiritual habits.

3. What Is in the Room?

We've already hinted at a big element that leads to the feel of the room—the stuff (or lack of stuff) in that room. But that stuff is important enough to warrant a bit more attention.

Simply put, the place for your spiritual habits needs to have **objects that nudge you toward those habits**. Remember in the last chapter how we talked about cues that you can "trip over"? The best cues are tangible and inviting, reminding you of the habit you're doing. You just feel drawn to them. *Those* are the physical objects you want in the room.

For instance, our friend Brian has a taper candle on the table where he prays. Before he begins praying, he lights the candle. When he's done, he blows it out. It's incredibly simple. But it's also beautiful, just enough of an enticement for him to want to sit and pray.

You might choose a candle, or a soft blanket, or a beautifully designed Bible, or a special pen you only use when reading the Bible. Make it personal to you, and make sure it's in the right spot.

The flip side of this is also the case: Make sure the wrong stuff stays out of the room. The fewer distractions around you, the more likely you'll be able to focus long enough to pray (or read the Bible, or whatever you're after). A television, for instance, probably isn't a great item to have in the room. Neither is your phone. The sheer sight of them cues your mind and body to start staring at screens.

Screens aren't the only agents of distraction, either. Your work bag may give you a visceral sense of stress, reminding you of upcoming assignments and unread emails. Your grocery list might make you wonder about upcoming meals you need to make. (*Did I already buy cilantro or was I supposed to do that today?*) A jumbled pile of your kid's schoolwork might be begging to be organized. Whatever it is, pay attention to which objects around you tend to distract you from prayer. And rather than relying on your willpower, keep those distracting items in their place.

SMALL STEPS YOU CAN TAKE TODAY

Bible Reading: We know God best by knowing His Word. Read it.

Like prayer, Bible reading can be overwhelming because of the sheer number of possible ways to do it. You can study it deeply or just read it quickly. You can meditate on it or memorize it. You can listen to the Bible (or a sermon) while you go for a walk. You can work through a Bible study or a Christian book with a group.

However you are reading the Bible, remember that the goal is to know God better. He wants to be with you, and in His Word, He is speaking. Your response is to *listen*.

Building a Bible-reading habit in the home—for families

- Make It Easy: The Bible is intimidating, but fortunately, there are a lot of great age-appropriate adaptations. Pick one (like David Helm's *Big Picture Story Bible* or Sally Lloyd-Jones' *Jesus Storybook Bible*) and read one story a night. Bite-sized stories with a beginning and an end? That's easy. And if you have elementary readers, try Kaleidoscope Kids' Bibles.[6]

- Make It Tangible: Again, kids' resources already tend to get this right. But make sure to choose a Bible that is inviting, the kind a kid would want to pick up.

- **Pick a Place: Where do you and your kids already gather? Their bedroom at the end of the day? The breakfast table? Choose the place that already slows everyone down and has you together. That's where you should put your Bible.**

Building a Bible-reading habit in the home—for grown-ups

- Make It Easy: Decide what you are going to read. Just about any reading plan will work. Just pick one—and make sure the pace starts small. You can always increase it.

- Make It Tangible: You probably already have a Bible you got for free somewhere. It's probably hideous. If you don't already have one, go get a beautiful Bible that you actually want to hold.

- **Pick a Place: Put the Bible where you will read it. Make sure you pass it at the right time and that the chair you have it by is good for reading. Your place doesn't have to be magnificent to become holy. But it does need to be intentional. Plus, don't be frustrated if you have to change the place a few times. Trial and error is part of the process.**

Choose Your Timing

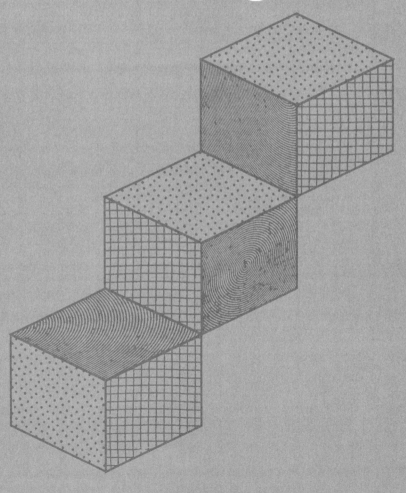

CHAPTER SIX

Question: Do you have a specific time set to start this habit?

Our "small step" suggestion: Pick a time and start, because restarting is always an option.

When picking the right time . . .

1. Day to day, prioritize evenings and mornings.

2. Season to season, pay attention to temporal landmarks.

3. Embrace the grace of the restart.

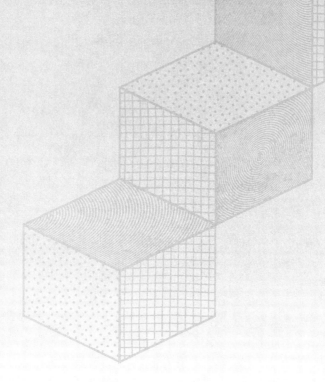

Magic in the Mist

am writing this chapter during October in North Carolina. Most days are still warm, but the mornings and evenings are pleasantly cool. It's sweatshirt weather. Fuzzy-sock weather. Firepit weather.

On some mornings, while I'm standing around waiting for my kids' school bus, I can begin to see my breath. Tiny puffs of air, usually invisible, hang in front of my face for a moment, then gradually disappear. My kids seem to have forgotten this magic existed last year, because it's just as surprising to them now as it was the first time they saw it.

"Daddy, Daddy, look! I can see my own air!" Teddy yells. He opens his mouth wide, issuing out short "ha" noises.

"It's *breath*," his older sister Lottie replies. But she quickly moves on from correcting her brother to making herself into a steam engine, puffing little bursts of air upward while she shuffles her feet forward.

Watching them mesmerized by the sight of their own breath, I'm mesmerized by the magic of it again, too. How fun, how rare, to get a glimpse of the invisible, if only for a moment.

The same dynamic happens, though with different senses, every time somebody speaks. Their vocal chords vibrate the air, which is why—momentarily—you can hear them. But at the moment you hear the words, the words themselves are gone. Like your cold morning bursts of breath, within a few seconds, there's no evidence those words were even spoken.

(I wonder if we would feel the same sense of magic about spoken words if we only heard them a few months out of the year, like early morning puffs of air?)

In the book of Ecclesiastes, the author compares our lives to a mist. The Hebrew word is *hevel*, usually translated as "vanity," "futility," even "meaninglessness." But the most literal translation of *hevel* is "vapor" or "mist." Like our breath in the morning, it's here for a moment, then gone. Like our words— vibrating in someone else's ears, then silent.

We tend to think of mist-life as depressing and sad—a common conclusion if you read Ecclesiastes over and over again. But in God's economy, life among the mists doesn't have to be a downer. It is simply a result of living as time-bound people. In fact, we can do more than merely accept the limits of our mist-life; we can even celebrate those limits as one of God's gifts.

To imagine mist-life as a gift, just think about music. Music itself requires that some sounds fade before others emerge. If every note came at you simultaneously, you wouldn't experience music; you'd only experience noise. For music to delight the senses, certain sounds must fade away so that others can take their place.[1]

What is true of music is true of all of life. We need experiences, like a music note, to fade away and make way for the new.

All of us live life among the mists. We are time-bound creatures who have never known life apart from time. And yet we all find it a bit unnatural. We comment on time's oddness, well, all the time. *Is it only two thirty? Wow, have we been in this house a year already? Where does the time go? Seems like the days keep moving faster. I can't believe she's graduating already.* You'd think we'd be used to it by now.

Time feels like an enemy to many of us. There is never enough of it, and it's always running out. God may tell us that our lives are a mist, but that hardly sounds like good news to us.

But God never reminds us of our mist-life to make us despair. He reminds us of our mist-life so we can walk at His pace, in His grace. He reminds us of our mist-life so we can celebrate the resurrection-life just around the corner.

If we learn to keep time in God's way, we can learn, like my kids, to see the magic in the mist.

DON'T START WITH "WHAT?" START WITH "WHEN?"

My goal here isn't to resolve the mysteries of space-time for you. (For that, watch a marathon of Christopher Nolan movies.) My goal is to help you take some steps forward in your spiritual habits. And for that, the main thing you need to know is: Timing matters.

When you're trying to grow in a particular spiritual habit, chances are you think a lot about the "what" (or its close cousin, the "how"). *What Bible reading plan should I choose? How should I pray? What am I allowed to do (and not do) during Sabbath? What is fasting supposed to look like?* These are important questions. But just as important is the question of "when."

In our experience, false starts in spiritual habits are just as likely to be about timing as the habits themselves. Sure, you may set yourself up to fail by choosing impossible goals—say, memorize the book of Romans in a week. That's a "what" mistake. But on the timing side, you can also set yourself up to fail by something as mundane as beginning a new Bible reading plan *on a Thursday.*

Starting the right spiritual habit at the wrong time can torpedo your good intentions. It's like trying to join in with a symphony a couple measures in. Possible, but awkward. But with the right count-off, you can enter into a spiritual rhythm on the right beat—at God's pace, in God's grace.

There are a few keys to starting your spiritual habit at the right time. Let's look at three:

1. Day to day, prioritize evenings and mornings.
2. Season to season, pay attention to temporal landmarks.
3. Embrace the grace of the restart.

1. Day to Day, Prioritize Evenings and Mornings

Imagine it's Saturday morning, around nine thirty. You've slept in longer than you have in years. (If you're a parent, remember, we're *imagining* here.

Go with me.) You wake up to a breakfast sandwich and some fresh fruit from your favorite restaurant.

How do you feel?

Now let's go somewhere else—actually, some*when* else. Imagine it's a Tuesday afternoon, around two thirty. You had an early lunch (leftover pasta), and your belly is telling you that you really should have had more protein. You've just finished an hour-long meeting at work, which you suspect could have been fifteen minutes. Or an email.

How do you feel?

I'll bet you imagined yourself in a much better mood in scenario 1 than scenario 2. (If the opposite is true . . . just, *how*?) We've all felt the sluggishness of the afternoon slump. Most of us power through with a second, or third, or fourth cup of coffee. We make do. But we wouldn't say we *love* midafternoon.

On the other hand, some societies lean into the afternoon slump, giving it space by closing down shops, even entire city blocks. *Siesta,* anyone?

It turns out that the afternoon slump is more than just a small inconvenience. Scientifically, it's been proven to frame much more of our day than we realize. As Daniel Pink notes in his book *When: The Scientific Secrets of Perfect Timing,* good things really do happen more often in the morning than in the afternoon: Social media posts are more positive; people are more likely to tell the truth; judges are less likely to pass harsh sentences; doctors are more likely to diagnose accurately.[2] And mistakes—often costly ones—happen much more often in midafternoon.

Doesn't that make you feel better about your productivity (or lack of it) last Tuesday at two thirty?

As a general rule, most people experience a U-shaped mood throughout their day: They begin relatively high, dip somewhere in the afternoon, and experience a second wind later in the day. In Daniel Pink's language, there's a peak, a trough, then a smaller rebound.[3]

That U-shape is pretty consistent for most people. What changes are the start times and the relative movement of each "peak." Early birds, for instance (this is Clayton and me), get a big boost as soon as their eyes open—often hours before dawn. They experience the afternoon trough like the rest of humanity, then have a smaller bump as the sun sets. By 9:00 p.m., though, there's not much usefulness from an early bird.

Night owls, on the other hand, have a later start time to their peak—say, nine or ten in the morning. And that first peak isn't as pronounced. They, too, dip (in both energy and mood) in midafternoon. Then they rally late in the day. But their rally is *big*, often carrying them far into the night. For night owls, 9:00 p.m. is a glorious time.

Most of us live somewhere in the middle of that spectrum—what Daniel Pink calls "third birds."[4] But the mood and energy pattern is the same throughout the day: High, low, high.

You might be able to guess what this means for spiritual habits. But hold that thought. Because Daniel Pink (as much as we love him) only wrote about these rhythms; he didn't create them.

God invented the morning and evening.

The Bible starts with the famous story of God creating the universe. For six days, God speaks—and from those words, entire worlds are formed. How different is God's speech from our own! Our words disappear, like mists, into the air. But His words are powerful and enduring, more solid and concrete than anything we've ever built—or ever could build. God's words bring order out of chaos, light out of darkness, beauty out of brokenness.

One of the most striking elements of the Genesis 1 creation story is the poetic repetition of key phrases. "And God said . . . " "And it was so." "And God saw that it was good." But one phrase appears a lot that, frankly, I didn't see the relevance of until very recently. It's the closing line for every day: "And there was evening, and there was morning."

We tend to skip over that phrase. It's too obvious. *Of course* there was morning and evening each day. And it's too mundane. In the context of God creating solar systems with a single exhale, why pause to point out that days have mornings? We already know that, and it's not that remarkable.

Yet there is a beautiful truth here we sorely need: Our mornings and our evenings aren't accidental moments. They are the God-given beats to our day, the rhythm He gave us from the beginning of time. Note that God didn't invent minutes or seconds—or even hours. Humans did that. God invented days. And He marked the days intentionally, morning and evening. Sunrise and sunset.

Except, if you're a close reader, you'll see that I've gotten the order backward. You and I imagine our day as beginning in the morning and ending in the evening. But God's start time is different. According to Genesis 1, the day begins as the sun descends—evening first, *then* morning.

Because of Genesis 1, the traditional Jewish conception of the day followed this evening-first pattern, with sunset marking the transition from one day to the next. This became one of the ways they expressed their trust in God. Rather than beginning the day with work, Jews begin their day by going to bed. Their work flows out of their rest, rather than rest being a reward for their work.[5]

And who was working the entire time, all through the night? God. Even in the shape of our days, *God starts*. When we awake every morning, we actually enter God's midday. And while He has work prepared for us, we aren't starting anything from scratch. We are responding to His gracious first move.

While we were unconscious and dreaming, He was beginning the day without us, working just as masterfully as He did when He spoke creation into existence. And every morning, we awake by that same power.

What does this mean for our spiritual habits?

Now, what does all of this have to do with our attempts to develop spiritual habits in the day-to-day?

We think it is prudent to pay attention to both the science and the theology of timing. If God designed daily and seasonal rhythms, we should try to dance along with those rhythms. If God gives newness every morning and the ability to wake in His power, we should work within that design.

We've got three ideas.

First, recognize that mornings and evenings are, in general, the most significant times of day. Yes, of course, two thirty in the afternoon might end up being the time you get engaged, or have a kid, or lose a loved one, or hear life-changing news. We're not saying *nothing* of significance happens in the afternoon. But God Himself marked the days by saying, "evening and morning." So if you're looking to start a new spiritual habit, evening or morning are good bets.

Second, as an embodied human, your circadian rhythms matter. We can't tell you what exact form your U-shaped energy takes on any given day. You might already know. If not, it's worth the time to figure it out. When do you find it easier to focus? When does your energy drag? Productivity gurus love talking about "managing your energy, not your time." It's a great principle, but the end goal is generally just to get more stuff done. Why not take that same idea and channel it toward developing a healthy spiritual life, too?

Just last week, for instance, I met with someone from our church who thought he had a spiritual problem. His Bible reading was stale. He knew he should love the Bible, but he was struggling to stay focused. I asked more about it, and it turned out that he was reading the Bible just before bed, as he always had. But while that had worked for him in college (when he had more energy), it wasn't working now. He found himself falling asleep the moment he opened the Bible. The solution we came to wasn't spiritual, but practical: Try reading the Bible when you aren't super sleepy.

Third, slow your pace. Remember, when God created the rhythms of our lives, He didn't invent minutes and seconds—as helpful as those time markers are. He framed our lives in the more gracious rhythm of morning and evening, day to day. *He prefers to work slowly,* so He wants us to move *at His pace.* Life in the twenty-first century feels frantically fast. We pack our schedules to the brim. We rush from one moment to the next. We move faster than ever, and we mean literally—in an age of horse-drawn carriages, who could have even imagined going as fast as each of us do on the interstate every day?

We don't have to abandon modern technology and ditch our cars (though a bit of a break from each isn't a bad idea). But we should recognize that God's intended rhythm to our days most likely feels more gracious than our own. Walking at God's pace, in God's grace will likely mean we move slower.

This also means—and we find this as tough as you do—*we get less done*. Creating space, daily, for spiritual habits often means we displace other things we could be doing. My time in prayer *could* be spent getting more work done. My time reading Scripture *could* be spent watching highlights from last night's game. It's not that work and sports are the enemy. But if we try to *add* spiritual habits to our days while still keeping those days packed with every other hurried activity, it just won't fit. You aren't a time-bender. You get one morning each day, one evening each day. Embrace that God-given limit and learn to walk in His grace, at His pace.

Alright, so that covers a single *day*. But timing matters just as much in the bigger chunks, too. So let's talk about the week, the month, and the year.

Celebrate What Is Already Working

Have you heard of "habit stacking"? Habit stacking is a method of pairing a new or difficult habit with an existing or easier one. Essentially, you put what you *want* to do with what you already *have* to do. I'll bet you already do this with some tedious chores in your life. Maybe while watching TV (want to), you also fold laundry (have to). Or you listen to a podcast (want to) as an incentive to go for a run (have to).

You're already habit stacking. So give yourself credit for it. You know what you're doing. Now, try to think up some spiritual habit stacks to add to the mix.

James Clear puts it this way: "The habit stacking formula is: After [CURRENT HABIT], I will [NEW HABIT]."[6]

It could look like this:

- After **I drink my coffee**, I will **say a two-sentence prayer.**
- When **I pull into my driveway**, I will **thank God for one good thing.**
- After **I brush my teeth**, I will **read one proverb.**

2. Season to Season, Pay Attention to Temporal Landmarks

Have you ever been to the gym the first week of January? For years I hadn't. I wasn't actively avoiding it; it just never (ahem) worked out. But then, a few years back, our family decided to head to the YMCA on New Year's Day. Want to guess who I saw there?

Everyone.

It was like an indoor block party. Every machine was occupied. The music was blasting. Strangers high-fived each other as they walked to the water fountains. Somewhere in the distance, I could have sworn I saw a disco ball appear. The air was thick with optimism and sweat.

None of this should have surprised me. But it did. I had assumed that the New Year's resolution was on its way out. Not dead, exactly, but at least on life support. And yet, the YMCA reminded me that the January 1 restart is still going strong.

Going strong . . . until it trips and falls. Because whether you love New Year's resolutions or not, you probably know how most of them end. With a resonant *thud*. Visit your local gym, say, on February 22 and take note—the wonder has left the building.

We're not sure how you feel about New Year's resolutions. You might despise them. Us? We love them. There's just something about turning the calendar that feels like a natural moment of possibility. The past 365 days may have been filled with mistakes, regrets, bad habits. But the 365 blank days staring back at us? Well, they're like a freshly fallen snow: None of them have been touched at all. Hope springs eternal.

Rationally, we know that change is difficult and hard-fought. We've seen enough Februarys to have a voice in our heads reminding us, *Don't get too excited*. But all of this rationality can't stop us. At a gut level, every January, something in us says, *This year can be different*.

It turns out we're not alone.

Social scientists have noticed that most of us, intuitively, have a felt sense of optimism at key moments on the calendar. They call these moments "temporal landmarks."[7] Just as we use physical landmarks to help us navigate our environment ("Turn left at the Shell station"), we create temporal landmarks to help us navigate time ("Let's connect again in the new year"). Temporal landmarks are those days when, metaphorically speaking, we can finally turn off the road we're on and head somewhere new.

The most obvious temporal landmark is the start of the year. But other "restart" dates trigger the same kind of response. Usually they are beginnings: It's that first day of summer break. The first day of the month. The first day of the week. The first day after a holiday.

Personal dates can become temporal landmarks, too. Your birthday is a temporal landmark. So is your anniversary. Or the first day of a new job. Or the first day back after a vacation.

When the calendar resets, people tend to think, *Maybe I can reset, too. Maybe I can start again*. And here's the thing: Science tells us that *we can*. When people attempt to begin new habits (or kill old ones) on temporal landmark dates, they are more likely to continue them later.

I know this has been true in my life. For instance, every November for the past decade, I've fallen off the pace in my running. (It's cold, it's dark. Look, winter is hard.) But just as reliably, every January, I pick up my running shoes again. Now, it's actually *darker* and *colder* in January . . . but the reset date kick-starts the habit. And sure enough, I'm propelled to ten more months of consistent running. For me, that's a win.

Or I think of my dad. He smoked cigarettes for years prior to my birth—and several years after. Of course, he knew they were bad for him. But breaking bad habits is hard. Then, one year, he resolved to quit. When did he do it? July 20, 1994, the day I turned ten. It still took a ton of work, but he did it. And the date he started mattered.

You can probably think of similar examples in your life, moments when you've started something—or *re*started something—at a key moment on the calendar. The timing may not have been intentional, but we can assure you: It mattered.

God's temporal landmarks

Just as God gives us rhythm to our individual days, He provides rhythms for our weeks and months, too. The most significant one is called the Sabbath.

The Sabbath is the first spiritual practice we find in Scripture. God created Sabbath, ironically, when he *stopped* creating everything else (that is, *after* days 1–6 of creation). He didn't need to take a break. He wasn't tired. But He wanted to give our weeks the right kind of rhythm, the right kind of pace. So on day 7, he said, "Stop. Take a beat. Put your feet up. Rest." That's actually a pretty wonderful invitation. You can take a break.

In theory, most of us like the idea of Sabbath. It's an invitation to stop all of our good work and enjoy all of God's good work—just like God does. Stop and enjoy. Walk *at God's pace* and *in His grace*. Who wouldn't want that?

In practice, though, most of us approach Sabbath with a mixture of guilt and confusion. We don't know if we're doing it right. In fact, we're pretty sure we're not.

I find a lot of comfort in Jesus' approach to the Sabbath. Since He was the Creator of the Sabbath, He knew what it was for—not guilt and confusion, but rest and wholeness. In a world full of religious people asking themselves, "Am I doing this right?" in comes Jesus with a much different question: "Would you like to be made right?" For Jesus, Sabbath was an invitation to wholeness. In fact, it always had been.

In Sabbath, we hear God inviting us to a life of presence and joy. Instead of hearing an exasperated teacher saying, "Have you gotten it right yet?" we hear a gentle Father saying, "Would you like to be made right?"

Sabbath is the anchoring rhythm in Scripture. But there are other rhythms, too, growing out of the Sabbath pattern. Every seven years, for instance, the Jewish people were to practice a "sabbath year," letting their land rest before getting back to work. (This is where we get the contemporary idea of a "sabbatical.") And every *seven* seven years—that is, every forty-nine years—Israel was told to practice a Jubilee year. Jubilee was like a super-Sabbath: All debts were forgiven; all slaves were freed. It's impossible to imagine a more radical temporal landmark than that. What a restart!

Why did God put all of these restarts into the world? Why have seasons like this at all? Because we are misty creatures, always in need of chances to begin again. We need grace—not just every now and then, but in a regular, repeatable cadence.

Restarts tend to feel like failures. But in God's economy, that's not the main reasoning. Restarts are not primarily a sign of our failure. They aren't really about us at all. Restarts are primarily a sign of God's grace. He offers us restarts because *He is gracious* toward us. He expects restarts. Because He wants us to walk *in His grace,* He wrote restarts right into the script.

What does this mean for our spiritual habits?

What do temporal landmarks and Sabbaths and Jubilees mean for spiritual habits? We've got three ideas.

First, identify as many of the temporal landmarks as you can. And remember, temporal landmarks can be social (shared by everyone) as well as personal (unique to you). Socially, you can look to the start of each week, the start of each month, the start of each season, and the day after major holidays. Personally, look to your birthday, significant anniversaries, or other "restart" dates after major events in your own life.

For instance, Clayton has a peculiar saying that flows out of the personal landmarks of his life: "January starts in February." He says this because his family has a lot of birthdays in January. This makes January a ton of fun, but it also makes January a rough time to start new habits. Rather than insisting on starting something on New Year's Day, he identifies the time his family *feels* like the new year starts—February 1.

Second, start a new spiritual habit on a temporal landmark. The benefit here is that you don't have to wait too long before you encounter a temporal landmark. They come around at least every week. So pick the next temporal landmark and decide you'll start (or restart) your spiritual habit then.

Third, slow down to notice the unique elements of each season. The temporal landmarks we find in Scripture intentionally slow us down. Sabbath, for instance, is meant to pull the brakes on our otherwise full-speed lives. Holidays are meant to pull us out of our normal rhythm.

In other words, temporal landmarks help us live more present to the moment God has given us, rather than dwelling on the past or rushing into the future. They allow us to experience God's beauty in the mist-life we live. In this way, temporal landmarks—whether Sabbaths or holidays or something else altogether—can serve as spiritual habits in themselves.

Recently, we have found tremendous value in reflecting on what makes each month of the year distinct. The seasons, after all, are still *there*. Our challenge is to see them, to notice them. To notice the first spring blossoms. The last snowfall of the season. The last mowing of the lawn in autumn. Or the start of "firepit season."

Marking these moments is one way we can slow ourselves down, drawing us into what Eugene Peterson calls Jesus' "unforced rhythms of grace" (Matt. 11:28–30 MSG). When we make space to *notice* the seasons around us, we often find ourselves *engaging* in the moment God has given us.

Not every season is perfect and beautiful. Not every season seems significant. But the older I get, the more I want to be present for all of them. To be *100 percent here* for each moment, each subtle shift in my life.

Don't just use every holiday as an opportunity to blow through, catch up, and win more. Use temporal landmarks as moments of grace, chances to slow down and be present. In that way, these temporal landmarks can become, in themselves, a sort of spiritual habit.

3. Embrace the Grace of the Restart

We're hoping this chapter provides you with some incredibly practical next steps. But we want more than that: We want you to feel the freedom that God has woven into time. We want you to walk *in God's grace, at His pace.* And for that, you need one last piece of good news: you're going to fail.

You're going to fail. That may not sound like good news to you. But consider what the Christian walk is. We are not asked to perform at a certain level, looking up to God hoping He gives us a "good enough" score for heaven. We aren't performing at all. We're living as redeemed children of God, adopted into His family on Jesus' account. As the apostle Paul said, "If we are faithless, he remains faithful—for he cannot deny himself" (2 Tim. 2:13).

In the end, our spiritual habits depend less upon our perfect timing and more on Jesus' perfect love. Remember, *God wants to be with you.* That's the goal.

This is good news for those of us who have had our fair share of spiritual false starts. After all, what discourages us when we try to develop new spiritual habits is . . . *us*! We know ourselves too well. We know how many times we've failed. We know that the same person who is vowing to do better was just as sincere the *last* time he vowed to do better.

But walking with Jesus, we can be honest about our past failures without despairing of our future possibilities.

It's true: I may be bringing my same old self into a new year—the same old frustrations, same old anxieties, same old jealousies. But I am following a Savior who makes all things new. He meets my failed attempts with grace, encouraging me to come back again. He doesn't look at my last year with a scorecard, as I'm tempted to do, evaluating my wins and losses. Over the past twelve months of my life, He has a very different banner written for me: "You are a beloved child of God. *Come and be with me.*" And over the following twelve months, the banner is the same.

As you and I peer ahead to the next temporal landmark, we do so under the banner of eternal, unconditional, death-defying love. With a Savior like this, we are able to run back up and try that spiritual habit again, and again, and again—even if we keep on falling—because when we engage with Him, we fall into the arms of love.

SMALL STEPS YOU CAN TAKE TODAY

Examen: Reflection that leads to gratitude.

Examen is a practice of daily reflection, meant to lead us to gratitude toward the God who was present with us for all the moments of our day. For all that was good, we thank God for His goodness and His presence. For all that was hard, we bring it to God, remembering that He was present with us then, too.

Building an examen habit in the home—for families

- Make It Easy: Keep it incredibly short and don't force it. Sometimes you'll get a deep reflection; other times you'll hear about what your kid ate for lunch. Both are great.
- Make It Tangible: Get a reminder with a list of questions. If your family has tried "a high and a low" or "a rose and a thorn" at dinner, provide some physical object that reminds you to have this conversation.
- Pick a Place: We recommend the dinner table. It's a great place for conversation, and a natural time to reflect on the day. The bedroom at bedtime can also work. (But don't do both.)
- **Choose Your Timing: We think dinnertime is the best option for this one. Conversation is open and free-flowing. Your little ones are in one place with your undivided attention. Give this time a little cue toward reflection and you have yourself a spiritual habit.**

- Make It Easy: Your examen doesn't have to come out as a sermon or well-written blog post. God isn't judging your public speaking or your writing style here.

- Make It Tangible: Get a paper journal, and a nice one. We use a "five-year journal" so we can track our reflections year over year. But you don't have to go so big. Just keep the entries short—literally a sentence or two—so it doesn't feel daunting.

- Pick a Place: Comfy is the name of the game here. A comfy chair should work. Or even your bed. (It's even okay if you fall asleep while you're doing this. Grace!)

- **Choose Your Timing: Though we do know people who practice examen first thing in the morning, reflecting on the previous day, the most natural timing seems to be at the very end of the day. But feel free to get creative on the timing. And know that reflection can happen daily, weekly, monthly, and yearly. Carve out time to review what has happened over that time period. Celebrate God's faithfulness and presence every time you go to bed, flip a calendar, or have a vacation.**

Make It Playful

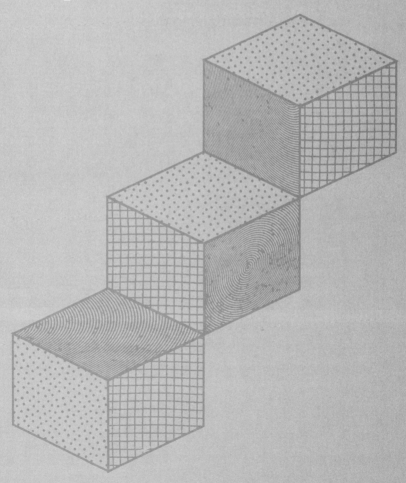

CHAPTER SEVEN

Question: Can you invite a seven-year-old to do your spiritual habit with you?

Our "small step" suggestion: Your spiritual habits should be simple and fun enough to invite your family into the fun.

1. Be playful in your spiritual habits. After all, play *is* a spiritual habit.

2. Say yes (in advance) to the playful moment.

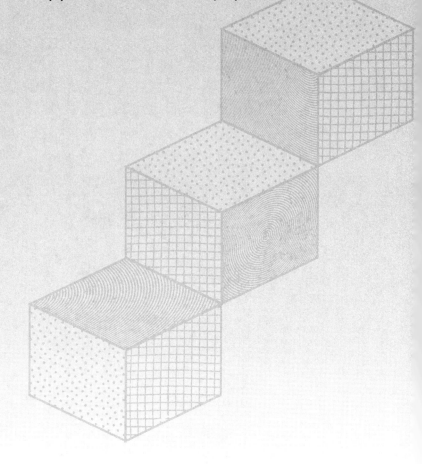

Jump Right in, the Water Is Freezing

A couple summers ago, Clayton was visiting our mutual friend Brian in Denver. Their two families were hanging out at a cabin on Lake Everist. The grown-ups were lounging in the hot tub, watching the kids, fifty feet away, as they played in the lake. The lake water, coming down from the higher mountains, was brisk, even for kids (they literally call it "snowmelt"). So they alternated between splashing up to their knees, then running and screaming back to the shore.

It was a pleasant enough moment. But then someone took the placid scene and ratcheted it up to eleven.

Without warning, six-foot-three Brian came barreling down toward the lake's shoreline, his Fabio-hair blowing in the breeze. None of the kids even saw him coming. In a flash—and in a splash—Brian had performed an epic belly flop into the frigid water.

The entire scene erupted. The parents, safely watching from the hot tub, applauded and cheered. The kids, who ten seconds before had only been dipping their toes in the water, screamed and piled on Brian, who spent the next few minutes tossing them, left and right, into the air.

It was, by everyone's account, the best moment of the entire trip.

At the time, Clayton couldn't quite articulate why. But now we've come to realize something surprising: Brian's belly flop wasn't just silly; it was spiritual.

WHY SO SERIOUS?

Here's an oddly controversial opinion: We think play is a good thing.

Does that sound obvious to you? Us, too. Honestly, we have a hard time thinking of anyone who is *opposed* to play and fun. And yet, for most of the grown-ups we know, play feels like a thing of the past. We can't be the only ones who look around and think, *Hey, everyone . . . what happened to recess?*

Most of us know that we used to play more than we do now, but we assume the downward trend is the inevitable result of becoming an adult. *Of course* we played more when we were seven than we do now that we're thirty-seven. We didn't have any responsibilities then! When you're seven years old, assuming you have a relatively safe environment, play comes as naturally as breathing. Your biggest responsibility on any given day is finishing a homework sheet or cleaning your room. There's room to roam, room to play.

But as you get older, you gradually accrue responsibilities. You have bills to pay. You have a job. You have kids of your own. You have to fix the washing machine. Or maybe call somebody to fix it. Or maybe replace the daggum thing. How much will that cost, anyway?

Ugh. It's a lot of work.

Becoming an adult—or, as our generation has playfully rebranded it, "adulting"—really does carry a growing need for responsibility. We wouldn't want our accountant or mechanic having the work ethic and training of an elementary child. As a result, we've come to assume that real grown-ups don't have room for fun or play. Play is a frivolous luxury, only available to kids . . . or people who insist on *acting* like kids.

In her book *The Power of Fun: How to Feel Alive Again,* science journalist Catherine Price captures this grown-up situation well: "We think that if we're focused on fun, we're not paying enough attention to the world's problems or doing enough to help other people."[1] There are serious problems all around us. So we had better become serious people to fix them. And serious people don't make room for play.

Or do they?

HOW DID WE GET HERE?

The anti-play bias we all sense as adults wasn't a foregone conclusion. Psychologist Mike Rucker, in his book *The Fun Habit: How the Pursuit of Joy and Wonder Can Change Your Life*, identifies our current mood as a combination of two historical streams—the American Dream and the Protestant work ethic.

The American Dream is the notion that anyone in the United States can achieve success. It doesn't matter where you begin. All you need is grit and hard work, and you can make it to the top. Whether you agree with the underlying premise or not (and there's good reason to view it with at least a dash of skepticism), we have to acknowledge that the American Dream still exercises a lot of power over us. For Americans, generally, hard work is not just a good idea, but a virtue.

If you add a religious element to the American Dream, you end up with the Protestant work ethic. (Technically, this is chronologically backward, since the secular American Dream is best understood as a later offshoot of the Protestant work ethic.) In the Christianity of the early United States, hard work was more than a virtue: It was evidence of God's saving power. Those who didn't work hard had reason to doubt whether they were true Christians. In a context like this, work was holy, and anything that distracted from work—say, fun—wasn't just worthless. It was sinful, evil, even demonic.[2]

Few of us would say, in so many words, that we overwork because of the American Dream or the Protestant work ethic. We simply sense, in our heart of hearts, that *we have to keep grinding*. Whether we're working as investment bankers or staying at home with three children, we get the feeling that *what we do* defines *who we are*. Through our work, our self-worth is on the line.

And this, I propose, is why play feels so out of reach to most of us. In a world of constant striving, all of us are reaching out to touch the bar of perfection. And as Catherine Price reminds us, "Perfectionism doesn't leave space for playfulness."[3]

We believe there is another way, a better way, than the serious path of perfectionism. Seriousness grows from the root of perfectionism. But play-fulness has another root.

THE (SURPRISINGLY VIRTUOUS) ROOT OF PLAYFULNESS

We Americans may have perfected the oppressive art of perfectionism, but we certainly didn't invent it. If you were to travel back to first-century Israel, you'd find another group of hardworking religious people known as the Pharisees.

The Pharisees (who we met back in chapter 3) were the preeminent religious leaders for God's people, known for taking God's laws seriously. They were so serious about God's law that they actually invented *other* laws to prevent them from breaking the 613 laws they already had. Seems responsible enough. After all, what could be wrong about taking God's very serious laws very seriously?

But you don't have to read far in the Gospels to realize that Jesus never seemed particularly pleased with the Pharisees. The feeling was mutual. The Pharisees didn't like how Jesus healed people on the Sabbath, for instance, which certainly seemed like it broke the rules. And Jesus had a persistent tendency to draw in all the wrong sorts of people—prostitutes and lepers and foreigners—the sorts of people who either didn't know or didn't care about the 613 laws.

Now, it's important to keep in mind that Jesus wasn't on a mission to simply throw out the old rule book. "Do not think that I have come to abolish the Law or the Prophets," He said. "I have not come to abolish them but to fulfill them" (Matt. 5:17). When it came to God's laws, Jesus was just as serious as any Pharisee.

But Jesus recognized that the Pharisees, with all of their zeal, had missed something essential. Listen to how starkly He put it:

"Woe to you, scribes and Pharisees, hypocrites! For you tithe mint and dill and cumin, and have neglected the weightier matters of the law:

justice and mercy and faithfulness. These you ought to have done, without neglecting the others. You blind guides, straining out a gnat and swallowing a camel!" (Matt. 23:23–24)

Ouch. No wonder the Pharisees weren't fond of Jesus.

The Pharisees, it seems, had become very meticulous about keeping the law, even to the point of giving 10 percent (that's what the word "tithe" means) of their spices to God. They had built a pretty impressive structure of perfectionism. But the roots were all wrong—injustice rather than justice, self-indulgence rather than mercy, pride rather than humility (Matt. 23:12, 23, 25).

The Pharisees had reached for perfect obedience. But it was a perfectionism growing from pride, so the fruits were rotten.

In contrast, Jesus showed a radically different way to become perfect:

At that time the disciples came to Jesus, saying, "Who is the greatest in the kingdom of heaven?" And calling to him a child, he put him in the midst of them and said, "Truly, I say to you, unless you turn and become like children, you will never enter the kingdom of heaven. Whoever humbles himself like this child is the greatest in the kingdom of heaven." (Matt. 18:1–4)

The doorway to the kingdom of heaven is wide open to children. Remember the "radical democracy" we mentioned in chapter 3? In God's kingdom, *everyone* is invited to sit at the king's table. It was—and is—the most radically democratic invitation the world has ever known. Pharisees didn't have a place for kids at their table. But Jesus put a kid right in the middle and said, "Be like him."

If our spiritual habits don't have a place for children, they aren't *Christian* habits.

Let's look closely, though, at what Jesus thought was so great about acting like a child. "Whoever *humbles* himself like this child . . ." What Jesus loved about children wasn't their innocence or their cuteness or their optimism. What He loved was their *humility*.

The foundation of perfectionism, shown by the Pharisees, was pride. But the foundation of playfulness, shown by these anonymous children, was humility.

This is why play is more than just a pastime or a hobby. Play is itself a spiritual habit, because the root of playfulness is humility.

What would it look like if we took Jesus seriously here?

As I write this chapter, I'm thirty-nine years old. If I'm following Jesus, that means I should be as wise as a thirty-nine-year-old *and* as trusting as a nine-year-old. I want both of these to be true of me—to be as steady as a thirty-nine-year-old and as emotionally expressive as a nine-year-old. I want to be serious when it's called for. But I also want to be childlike enough to humble myself when serious *isn't* what's called for.

The way to manage both of these together isn't primarily to act like you're an elementary school kid. It's to embrace humility. It's to make yourself smaller.

G. K. Chesterton once quipped, "How much larger your life would be if your self could become smaller in it."[4] There's some great insight there. Making yourself smaller doesn't necessarily make you *lesser*. It makes the world around you *greater*, more full of wonder and delight. And when you're surrounded by wonder and delight, play is much more natural.

Not many of us think of humility as a fun endeavor, but it can be. Play can be an avenue to greater humility, because it reminds us that we're more like little kids than we are like all-powerful gods.

This isn't to say that humble people are inherently silly. The truly humble person takes a lot in life seriously—just not everything. She is most likely serious about ideas, serious about other people, serious about her work. But she probably knows herself well enough to be tremendously un-serious about herself and much more likely to be playful.

To which we say, that's good. And good for her.

PLAY YOUR WAY TO HOLINESS

What's interesting to us is that social scientists, when reflecting on play, seem to identify a slightly different connection. We say, "Humility leads to play." The social scientists say, "Play leads to less self-consciousness"—which is to say, to humility. Play isn't just a product of humility; it seems to produce more of the humility we're after. It's a spiritually virtuous cycle.

And humility isn't the only benefit, either. Check out this laundry list of benefits from regular play:

- Play fosters greater empathy.[5]
- Play leads to increased creativity and innovation.[6]
- Moments of play are much more likely to be "memory-makers."[7]
- Play increases the capacity to connect relationally.[8]
- Play decreases people's self-consciousness, making them more aware of others than themselves.[9]
- Play makes people more resilient.[10]
- Play increases people's ability to be present in the moment.[11]
- Play makes people happier, healthier, and more productive.[12]

If we told you there was a spiritual habit that could increase your empathy, creativity, productivity, compassion, resilience, presence, and humility . . . wouldn't you say "Yes!"? This turns the Protestant work ethic on its head: Rather than play being a mark of sin, play becomes a spiritual habit in its own right.

Social worker, author, and speaker Brené Brown points out that we resist play because it seems so unproductive. Not only is this a false assumption (studies show that people who play frequently are *more* productive in their work, not less), it also reinforces a nasty spiral of production-driven identity. "In today's culture," Brown writes, "our self-worth is tied to our net worth, and we base our worthiness on our level of productivity."[13] We can't play because our very worthiness is on the line.

But play requires you to stop work.

Seen in this light, play is simply one of a dozen versions of *rest*. No wonder we don't play very much—as a culture, we don't *rest* very much. We don't get enough sleep. We don't step away from our work. We don't take real vacations. In Brown's words, we wear "exhaustion as a status symbol," because exhaustion means we're really productive people.[14] And being really productive people means we matter.

To all of this, Jesus says, "Turn and become like children" (Matt 18:3). Lay down your attempts to build your worthiness by how much you can get done, and be a child before your heavenly Father. *God wants to be with you*, so rest in Him. Feel the freedom to play with Him. And with others.

This may not come naturally to us. Play, after all, is a risky venture. It requires more than just humility—it requires vulnerability. Even the most playful person will suddenly become reserved when surrounded by strangers. And even the most reserved person can come to life in the presence of true friends. The beauty of walking with Jesus is realizing that the one person whose opinion matters most invites you to interact with Him like you're a little kid. You can be vulnerable, even playful, around God.

And, with the right habits in your life, you can build that kind of playful community around yourself, too. Authentic relationship feeds play; play feeds authentic relationship.

Celebrate What Is Already Working

Do you ever play with your kids? I'm guessing you do. Maybe not as much as you'd like. Certainly not as much as *they'd* like (it seems endless, sometimes, doesn't it?). But I'm guessing you play much more now than you did before you became a parent.

We believe that playing with your kids is a spiritual habit. You don't have to suddenly transform your games into "Christian" games for them to be spiritually significant. You just need to see the fun around you as a spiritual moment. It's not a distraction from your walk with Jesus. It's part of your walk with Jesus.

What is it for you? Kicking the soccer ball around? Giving piggyback rides? Playing *Yahtzee*? Singing karaoke? Building Legos?

Whatever play you're doing, own it as a spiritual habit. It's cultivating humility in you and making you vulnerable. It's providing a meaningful connection to another soul. So enjoy it.

Do more of it. And give yourself credit for it.

MAKE YOUR SPIRITUAL HABITS SIMPLE AND FUN ENOUGH TO INVITE YOUR FAMILY INTO THE FUN

At this point, you might be ready to get out there and play already. If so, don't let us stop you. This book will be here when you get back. But if you need a bit more of a kickstart to apply this to your spiritual habits, here are a couple of ideas.

1. Be Playful in Your Spiritual Habits

Spiritual habits are important. But they really don't have to feel like a trip to the dentist. They can be fun and fruitful at the same time.

For instance, you might decide to put down your grown-up Bible and read *The Jesus Storybook Bible* for a while—not for the kids, but for yourself. Maybe, if you want to cultivate a gratitude habit, instead of simply writing down three things a day you're grateful for, start each day with something really lighthearted that you're grateful for—a food you like or a song you've been listening to on repeat. Maybe try drawing or acting out a scene from the Bible.

Take the spiritual habits you have and ask yourself, *How would I modify this to fit a seven-year-old?* Then realize that what's great for a seven-year-old is also great for you.

You could even make your spiritual habits into a sort of game. We're not the first to come up with this idea: There's a current trend among productivity gurus called "gamification." In essence, you turn habits you want to cultivate—drinking more water, studying for an exam, doing the laundry—into little games for yourself. By translating a chore into a game, you're more likely to play your way through it.

We think this works with spiritual habits, too. In fact, gamifying spiritual habits is a beautiful way to counteract our tendency toward perfectionism. Because if you're playing a game, you have the freedom to mess up. You're actually expected to. But you also want to keep on playing.

How might you gamify a spiritual habit? Take a cue from the Bible app, which rewards you with streaks for consecutive days reading the Bible. Or use a tangible item—we use round wooden chips and a glass jar—to track the number of times you read the Bible or pray. The more the chips pile up in the jar, the more you feel like you're winning the game, even if you've broken the streak. You could even assign point levels to certain habits (+10 for every chapter of the Bible), or create time challenges you want to beat (*How long can I go with my phone off? Current record—two hours, forty-five minutes!*). Get creative and try not to let any pressure into it: What would make it fun *for you*?

2. Say Yes (in Advance) to the Playful Moment

Catherine Price points out that real play only happens "when it has space to unfurl."[15] Distraction and busyness kill any attempt at play. If we want play to be a regular part of our lives, we need to make space for it. We need to say "yes" to the playful moment *before* it shows up.

Ironically, one of the best ways to free ourselves up to say yes is by having clear times when we say "no." Creating boundaries between work and home allows people to be fully focused in both spheres, which is a win-win. You aren't likely to be available to play with your seven-year-old on a random Tuesday morning—she's in school and you're in a staff meeting. That's fine. But if it's Friday night at eight, the expectations had better be different. Unless it's truly an emergency, your boss shouldn't feel the liberty to reach out and expect a swift response. You're present with your kids, with your spouse. On Friday nights, they get your "yes" and work gets your "no."

"True fun," Price says, "occurs exclusively in the present tense."[16] It's an experience. It demands our active attention. And with our attention being as fractured as it is these days, couldn't we use that kind of nudge?

Where do we get that nudge?

None of us is as hooked on play as our kids are. Rather than seeing that as a problem, recognize it as a spiritual opportunity. It's an invitation into connection and presence. After all, so much of developing spiritual habits is learning to *pay attention*. In the battle to pay attention, your kids are your allies.

One of the best depictions we've seen of this is in the cartoon show *Bluey*. (I don't know how I even made it *this far* in the book without mentioning *Bluey*.) What makes the show so fun is that the parents, Bandit and Chilli, tend to "say yes" to fun in every single episode. Even if they only carve out a minute or two between their other responsibilities, they're available with a posture toward "yes." That "yes" doesn't create the hilarity that ensues—almost always Bluey and her sister Bingo do—but it creates the environment for it.

Or remember Brian's lakeside belly flop? Brian may have taken the biggest risk, but it's important to realize that he wasn't the first one in the water. The kids were. More often than not, kids are going to be the first to recognize an opportunity to play. So if you want to follow the fun, follow your kids.

Our kids are eager to invite us into their world of play. It's a world of delight, of silliness, of love . . . and of spiritual wealth. Play is a spiritual habit, and in our oh-so-serious grown-up world, it may be one of the most important.

So what should you do with that?

Remember what we said in chapter 3: Your "decision fuel" is burning. So decide *in advance* when you will say yes to play.

At some point in the next week, your kid is going to ask you to come play with her. What we're telling you is, "say yes." Say yes in advance, so when the interruption comes, you already know the answer. Even if it's just five minutes . . . say yes.

SMALL STEPS YOU CAN TAKE TODAY

Worship: Sing the truth about God.

Singing, like playing, is one of those essential human habits that we tend to take for granted. But it's no accident that songs play a major role in child education and development. Singing helps us remember, helps us connect, and even makes us feel happier. So it should not surprise us that songs sit at the center of Christian worship.

Building a worship habit in the home—for families

- Make It Easy: Thankfully, children's worship songs are already pretty easy. Chances are your kids learned the songs before you. So the toughest part will be *you* learning them! (But trust us, it won't be that tough.) Maybe even pick a playlist or an artist in advance.

- Make It Tangible: Children's worship songs often have hand motions that go along with them. Learn the motions and dance along. Get a Bluetooth speaker you don't mind leaving out in the room.

- Pick a Place: If you've got speakers, put them in the main area of your house. If you've got musical instruments (next level, look at you!), put *those* in the main area of your house. Make music part of the environment.

- Choose Your Timing: When your kids ask, say yes! Songs are the perfect length for a short break, so you can totally commit and still be finished in less than five minutes.

- **Make It Playful: Follow your kids' lead here. They may want you to sing in a silly voice. Go for it. They may want to use that obnoxious microphone their aunt got them last Christmas. Give it a whirl.**

Building a worship habit in the home—for grown-ups

- Make It Easy: Our churches have already made this one as simple as possible. Every single church we know uses music as part of the service. So go . . . and sing!

- Make It Tangible: If you can read music, get a copy of a hymnal. If you can play, make your instrument easily accessible. And if you can't do any of that, this is a moment where your phone may actually help you out—"favorite" a few worship songs so your music-streaming app starts sprinkling those into your regular mix.

- Pick a Place: Music can become an essential part of the environment for many of your spiritual habits. Consider using worship music along with your other spiritual rhythms (like prayer or Bible reading).

- Choose Your Timing: You probably already listen to music—in the car, at the gym. Rotate some worship music into the music you already listen to.

- **Make It Playful: Do you ever have a song stuck in your head? Throughout the day, you'll hum it to yourself. Well, rather than muttering it under your breath, really go for it. Sing out loud!**

Find Your Friends

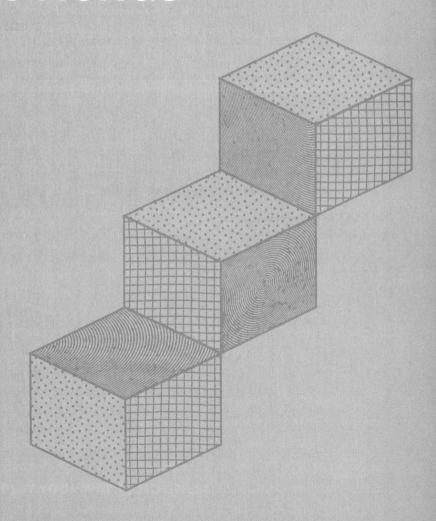

CHAPTER EIGHT

Question: Do you have a few friends that are doing this spiritual habit with you?

Our "small step" suggestion: You oughta. Friends help!

By way of review:

1. Make It Easy: Make it even easier than you think you need to.

2. Make It Tangible: Set a cue that means something to you.

3. Pick a Place: Pick a place that is inviting and free of distractions.

4. Choose Your Timing: Season to season, pay attention to temporal landmarks.

5. Make It Playful: Say yes (in advance) to the playful moment.

In Search of a Left Shoe

As a father to two elementary-aged kids, I am constantly struggling to get out the door on time. It doesn't seem to matter how much buffer time I leave for us—something always slows us down. A water bottle has gone missing. Or a left shoe. Or that special Spider-Man toy. Then, once I've located water bottles *and* shoes *and* Spider-Man, I've lost sight of one (or both) of my kids.

The end result? We always pile into the van about ten minutes later than I'd like.

In contrast, a few weeks ago, my wife took our kids to visit her sister, and I had a few hours to myself at the house. I remember a peculiar feeling, lacing up my shoes and walking out the door: *Wait . . . shouldn't I be doing something else?* It seemed almost too easy. I considered throwing one of my shoes under the car, just for a sense of normalcy.

You may not have the same get-out-the-door wrangle as me, but I'm sure you've felt it: Traveling alone is way quicker than traveling in a group. Multiply the number of people with you, and you're also multiplying how long it takes to mobilize that group.

But while it can feel freeing to go it alone, it's not nearly as meaningful. For instance, I could get to the Grand Canyon—or Paris, or Disney World—faster without anybody else with me. But why would I? The experience, though slower, would be much better enjoyed with people I love.

As the old adage goes, "If you want to go fast, go alone. If you want to go far, go together."[1]

When it comes to spiritual habits, Clayton and I are big "go far" people. The trouble is, we live in a "go fast" society. And the more pressure we feel to "go fast," the less likely we are to link arms with others in our spiritual journey. After all, other people are always looking for that left shoe or their Spider-Man toy—metaphorically speaking. Who has time for all that?

Well, for one, *you* do. You absolutely have time to join with other people on your spiritual journey. Because, if you don't make your spiritual journey a group effort, you're likely to go fast in the short run, but not very far in the long run. After all, we may live in a "go fast" world, but *God prefers to work slowly.* He lives in a "go far" world. We should, too.

For most of you reading this book, you've got years and years ahead of you. You don't need spiritual hacks to change the next few days of your life. You need to take consistent and small steps in your spiritual life, inching forward over decades, not days. You need habits that bear fruit over the next twenty years.

And for that, you need friends.

THE HABIT-HELPING POWER OF FRIENDS

Most of us are quite a bit more influenced by our peers than we'd like to think. We want to be freethinkers, "going against the flow." So we try to make choices that feel independent and unique. Sometimes we succeed. Most of the time, though, our actions are deeply indebted to the people around us. Only in retrospect—say, glancing through old photos—do we realize that we were buying and wearing and watching and eating what most people around us were.

If all of your friends eat tofu, chances are you're eating tofu. If all of your friends are watching *Bluey*, you're at least going to check it out—which you should, because it's amazing. The flip side of this is true, too: If none of your friends eat Taco Bell (or wear Crocs, or go to museums, or whatever), you're not likely to be the outlier that does. Not often, anyway.

Rather than fight against this (*I'm going to zig when everyone else zags!*), it's good to begin by simply recognizing it. Your close community shapes what you do. So enlist your friends as allies in your spiritual growth. And offer yourselves as allies to them, too. Remember, if you want to go fast, go alone; but if you want to go far, go together.

Social scientists have identified at least six ways in which other people positively shape our daily habits. When it comes to our habits, other people (1) increase our confidence, (2) give us encouragement, (3) provide accountability, (4) multiply our enjoyment, (5) fix our mistakes, and (6) give us a sense of purpose.[2]

Let's take a look at each of those benefits.

1. Friends Increase Our Confidence

In *Power of Habit*, Charles Duhigg writes, "People might be skeptical about their ability to change if they're by themselves, but a group will convince them to suspend disbelief. A community creates belief."[3] A fundamental ingredient in any change is belief: We've got to think change is actually possible. And the most surefire way to foster that belief is through seeing someone else live it out. It makes us say, "Oh, it really *is* possible. It really is true."

Being with a body of believers is a powerful agent to help us believe what we say we believe. The more other people remind us of what's true, the more likely we are to believe it—which increases our confidence in our spiritual habits.

2. Friends Give Us Encouragement

Not only do friends help us believe what we say we believe, they also give us boosts along the way. I can't even count the number of times I've attempted something difficult, simply because someone close to me said, "You've got this," or "I believe in you." The more other people encourage you—whether you're trying to bake a new recipe or trying to pray more consistently—the more likely you are to keep going.

3. Friends Provide Accountability

If I tell God I'm going to memorize Genesis 1, I may or may not follow through. But if I tell my coworker Pritesh that we're going to memorize Genesis 1 together, I'm more likely to do it. Odd how that works, isn't it? I suspect it's because *I can't see God.* But Pritesh? Well, I'll see him in the office on Thursday.

Accountability helps us in our habits, especially in the "mundane middle"—after the initial excitement has worn off, but before the long-term benefits seem evident. It's much tougher to flake on a workout program when that workout program is a team sport—other people are counting on you, so hitting snooze means you're sleeping in while your friends are running wind sprints. Solidarity pushes you to get out of bed.

4. Friends Multiply Our Enjoyment

Every October, our local city of Durham plays host to the Bull City Race Fest—a half-marathon and five-mile run (pick your poison). Like many road races, there are prizes for the first three men and women finishers. But hardly anyone runs it for the prize. So why do hundreds of people show up to run early on a Sunday morning?

Simple: Because hundreds of *other* people are showing up to run early on that Sunday morning.

Running alone can bring nearly all of the same benefits as running in a group. But it's just so much more *fun* to run through downtown with hundreds of people.[4] The same is true of spiritual habits, too. It's possible to have a great time all by yourself—say, reading your Bible, or practicing Sabbath. But more often than not, what transforms a good spiritual habit into a joyful moment is the presence of other people.

5. Friends Fix Our Mistakes

To grow in any habit, spiritual or otherwise, you need corrective feedback along the way. And few things are better for offering corrective feedback than other people.[5] They can help you see blind spots in your habit. They can share experiences that you lack. And they can do all of this with a supportive spirit. A great teacher or coach (or, if we're talking spiritual habits, a pastor) can offer insights and fix mistakes in our habits.

But better than a teacher, coach, or pastor is a peer, someone engaged in the same struggle as you. It's the kid sitting next to you in class, sharing how he worked through that same tough algebra problem. It's a fellow dad, sharing how many times he *tried* to start a family devotional with his kids, and all of the false starts he experienced along the way.

6. Friends Give Us a Sense of Purpose

Not only do friends make your habits better, friends also make your habits *matter*. They elevate your experiences, giving you a greater sense of purpose. In other words, friends don't just help with your habits; the act of friend-ing is itself a beautifully good habit.[6]

To feel this purpose, though, it's important that you and your friends literally occupy the same space at the same time. Virtual connections—whether over text or Zoom or social media—can be decent placeholders. But they pale in comparison to being in the presence of others. Practicing our faith face-to-face and shoulder to shoulder creates a sense of belonging and solidarity, and there's simply no virtual shortcut. As Justin Whitmel Earley puts it in his fantastic book *Made for People*, "Food alone is just a big meal, but friendships make a feast."[7]

Celebrate What Is Already Working

If you're like most Americans, you may not feel like you have a lot of friends. But you're a social creature, so I can guarantee you've got some.

If you aren't thrilled with the friend group you've got, it may be good to reset your expectations. Your friendships aren't like the ones you've seen on TV. But you know that's not real. They aren't like the friendships you see celebrated on Instagram. But that's fake, too. They aren't even like the friendships you had when you were twenty. But that was a very different phase of life.

Friendships can be messy and confusing and disappointing. And in our day, they are constantly changing. But they are also beautiful—and beautifully possible. You also don't need as many as you might think to radically change your life.

So take a look at the relationships you've got. Appreciate the good ones that God has given you. And keep it up.

GOD AND HIS FRIENDS

What social scientists have identified about companionship goes back much further than they might realize. In the very first story in the Bible, God looks at His brand-new creation, untouched by sin, and says, in essence, "Hmm, something's off."

Literally, what God says is, "It is not good" (Gen. 2:18). This is a huge deal, especially given how often the refrain of "God saw that it was good" shows up in the previous chapter—seven times! Over and over and over again, Genesis 1 paints the picture of God miraculously creating the universe. And His verdict over every piece of it is, "This is good!"

So what has changed from Genesis 1 to Genesis 2? Satan hasn't shown up yet. No one has sinned. So what's wrong?

Someone is alone.

In Genesis 2, the author zooms in on the creation of people, slowing the highlight reel for us to get a closer look. We read that God made Adam first, then Eve. But between Adam and Eve, God paused long enough to say, "It is not good that Adam is alone."[8]

Theologians have long struggled with this statement. How can a person, in God's very presence, without a hint of sin, be in a "not good" situation?

The answer comes from an unexpected place, the most fundamental and head-scratching doctrine of Christianity—the Trinity. The doctrine of the Trinity states that while there is only one God, this one God exists eternally as three distinct persons—Father, Son, and Spirit. It's a doctrine that makes our eyes blurry and our brains hurt (even, or maybe especially, those of us who have been to seminary for years). Most Christians, if they're honest, tend to ignore it. I understand the temptation.

This isn't the place to unravel all the mysteries of the Trinity for you.[9] But it's imperative that we not skip it. Because one of the most beautiful implications of the Trinity is this: God has never been alone.

At no point in God's existence did He exist as one person. From eternity past up until today, He has always been in loving friendship with Himself. Community is inherent to God. Which is why Scripture can say, "God is love" (1 John 4:8). Not just, "God *loves*," which is true. Not even, "God is *loving*," which is also true. But in His essence, forever and always, "God *is* love." Think about it: Love requires more than one. Because God is a Trinity, He has always embodied and experienced love, even before people came on the scene.

Even when it comes to friendship, God did it first! *God starts*—we simply respond.

Since God has always existed in a relationship of love, it helps explain why He could look on Adam, sinless but solitary, and say, "This isn't good." Because Adam, while sinless, was solo.

Friendship, then, isn't just a socially useful thing. It's certainly not a need we feel because of some deficit in ourselves. Quite the opposite. Friendship is part of what it means to be made in God's own image.

From the day Adam first opened his eyes until today, we humans have needed each other. All of us. And we always will.

Like many of you, I find this truth to be beautiful in theory but difficult in practice. I know that isolation is a major problem in our society. But more often than not, I find myself actively pursuing it. I seek more independence from others. Fewer weak moments. Being in community with other people, after all, is hard work. It requires time. People are messy. They are constantly losing their Spider-Man toy and their left shoe.

But you know what, for me, is even tougher than caring for other people? Receiving help *from* other people. It's humbling, and not in the Instagram, humblebrag kind of way (*Just got another promotion at work. #humbledbythis*). Relying on others isn't easy. I'd rather be a fully independent, self-sustaining adult. I don't want to *need* anyone. I want to be strong.

To which God says, "Sorry, bub, that's not how I made you. Even *I* don't operate that way." If interdependence isn't too good for a triune God, it shouldn't be too good for me, either.

This is such a counterintuitive truth for me that I repeat it to myself every day. Well, technically, I repeat it with my children. But it's just as much for my sake as theirs.

Every morning, as I drive them to the bus stop, I ask my children seven questions. It's a sort of mini catechism, grounding them in what's true as they begin their day. It's not particularly revolutionary—just seven simple questions to frame their day in God's love. And since we do it in the car, I call it our "car-techism." (I'm a dad. Dad puns just sort of happen, okay?)

The fifth question of the car-techism is, "Can you do what God wants on your own?" The answer? "No: I need other people and they need me."

I want interdependence to be the air my kids are breathing. For that matter, I want to breathe in that air, too.

FIVE SMALL STEPS TO HABIT-HELPING FRIENDSHIP

We recognize that more than any of our previous chapters, it can be challenging to put this one into practice: *Invest more in friendships*. Yeah, thanks. That's simple advice, but it's certainly not easy.

So here's what we're going to do. We're going to walk back through the five steps we've already covered—Make It Easy, Make It Tangible, Pick a Place, Choose Your Timing, and Make It Playful—and we're going to see what it looks like to add friendship into the mix. We believe that each of these principles can feed true friendship *and* that friendship can help foster these five steps.

What we've provided here are five small steps—small decisions you can make today for "go far" kind of change tomorrow. If what we suggest doesn't fit your context, peek back at those pages yourself and make your own connections. We'll bet you can pretty easily see how adding another person or two sparks some new ideas.

1. Make It Easy . . . with Friends

Back in the "Easy" chapter, we said:

- **Forgive yourself:** Don't listen to influencers (much).
- **Make it easier than you think:** Don't just start with easy. Start with easier—much easier—than you think you need to.
- **Write it down:** Decide up front on the what, the where, the when, the who.

Let's pick up that second idea: **Make it even easier than you think you have to**. The task of building friendships is intimidating. Sure, all of us would love the sort of friends who show up when we are in the hospital, or who watch our kids for free (just because they love us). But that's a significant level of commitment. Right now you're struggling to even meet up with a friend for coffee.

Don't let the beautiful vision of friendship scare you away from a small step you can take today. You can start with a target—say, sharing a meal with a friend once a week. But break that target down to an even easier step: *Invite* a friend to a meal once a week. Even if you don't make it happen this week, you've started some movement. You're on your way.

2. Make It Tangible . . . with Friends

Here was our advice on the "Tangible" side of things:

Set a cue that:

- . . . you can touch.
- . . . you trip over.
- . . . distracts you from your phone.
- . . . works for you, not for us.

Try that last one on for size. Specifically, **set a cue that means something to you.** Tangible objects often remind us of other people. For instance, I have a nifty space pen (yes, I am a nerd) that I use for journaling. This pen was a gift from a friend, and I think of him every time I use it. Because of that, every now and then, I'll text him to let him know I'm thinking of him. The tangible object not only reminds me of my friend but helps cultivate another connection with him.

You probably don't have a pen as your cue. But other meaningful gifts from one friend to another can act as spiritual reminders, nudging our minds to think of that other person. Maybe it's a sweatshirt, or a book, or a picture on your desk, or even an old-school friendship bracelet. When a physical object reminds us of the love of another person, that's a win. If it reminds you to reach out, even better.

3. Pick a Place . . . with Friends

When it comes to "Place," this was our digest:

- **Where is the room?** Pick a place you pass often.
- **What does the room feel like?** Pick a place that is inviting and free of distractions.
- **What is in the room?** Pick a place that has the right items in the room.

Let's try out the second one here: **Pick a place that is inviting and free of distractions.** Spending time together with others is important. But not all shared time is equal. And an inviting environment often makes all the difference. As Mike Rucker points out in *The Fun Habit*, one of the essential ingredients of friendship is "a setting that helps us relax and let down our guards."[10]

A few months ago, I was sitting around a backyard fire with a couple friends. We were enjoying the cool evening, catching up on life and leisurely getting to the important bits of the conversation. But then the weather changed. In the span of five minutes, the skies opened up, extinguishing the fire and forcing us to scramble to my garage.

We plopped down in our camp chairs and tried to pick the conversation back up. It was . . . okay. But something significant had changed. Rather than sitting around a warm fire, mostly in the dark, we were now in the bold and cold fluorescent lighting of my garage.

A garage is a great safe haven from rain, but it doesn't usually spark deep connections between friends. So be intentional with your shared space. Aim for coffee shops, campfires, or lakeside walks.

4. Choose Your Timing . . . with Friends

How does "Timing" affect our spiritual habits? Behold:

- Day to day, prioritize **evenings and mornings**.
- Season to season, pay attention to **temporal landmarks**.
- Embrace the **grace** of the restart.

We especially like the second one here: **Season to season, pay attention to temporal landmarks**. Starting new spiritual habits is hard. *Re*starting spiritual habits you once did can often be harder. But there's something about those restart dates—like New Year's or the beginning of the school year—that gives us fresh life. On one of those restart dates, you aren't the only one trying to start over. A lot of people are. So take advantage of that.

In *The Power of Moments*, Chip and Dan Heath say that one of the most important ways to knit people together is by "creating a synchronized moment."[11] Don't just start a new Bible reading plan. Start that Bible reading plan *at the same time as your roommate*. Don't just start turning your phone off during the Sabbath. Turn it off *on the same day as your friend*. Sync up the start—you'll not only be more likely to keep going; you'll also increase your chances of knitting your heart with someone else's.

5. Make It Playful . . . with Friends

Our advice back in the "Playful" chapter boiled down to:

- **Be playful** in your spiritual habits.
- **Say yes** (in advance) to the playful moment.

We'll go with the second one this time: **Say yes (in advance) to the playful moment.** Not just with your kids, but with the other grown-ups in your life.

If you're driving to lunch and your friend says, "Ooh, I *love* this song," then turn up the volume and sing along. Or if someone asks you to dinner, try as hard as humanly possible to say "yes." There will always be some other thing competing with that time. Try to keep that other thing at bay. After all, opportunities for fun don't present themselves terribly often. If you don't prioritize fun moments with your friends, chances are your schedule will fill up.

I know that prioritizing fun isn't easy. In any given moment, there's always more work to be done somewhere. But while I've often regretted working too much, I've never regretted saying yes to a fun and meaningful moment with others. And when I reflect on the highlights of my days, weeks, and years, fun moments seem to rise to the top.

You don't have to play for hours every day to make a meaningful moment with a friend. You just need to be ready to say "yes" when it comes.

DECADES, NOT DAYS

So, dear reader, we'll ask you the same car-techism question I ask my kids: *Can you do what God wants on your own?*

You've already read this chapter, so you know our answer: *No. You need other people and they need you.*

Do you believe that? We hope you do. Not because it's the "right" answer. Certainly not because we want you to feel guilty. We hope you learn to lean into friendships because it's how God made you, because it's how God Himself operates. *God starts* the process of friendship—and now He invites you to join Him.

We know friendships aren't easy. Lost friendships still make your heart ache. Your social media "friends" are many, but you sense that true friends are few. Other people seem to be having plenty of fun with their friends, while you're just struggling to take care of your two preschool kids.

We get it.

But you don't have to bear the whole burden here. The same God who looked at Adam and said, "It's not good for this guy to be alone," immediately went to work to solve the problem. God doesn't just tell us to love each other; He also provides the power for us to do it. We believe friendship is so valuable to God that He will meet your small attempts and multiply them.

Friendship, like all spiritual habits, is worth celebrating, even in its most feeble forms. Start with that. Thank God for the relationships you do have.

And then remember that friendship—again, like all spiritual habits— bears fruit over decades, not days. You can make a few small steps today. You may not go fast. But we believe you'll go far.

SMALL STEPS YOU CAN TAKE TODAY

Friends: Community can be messy and confusing and beautiful and fun—but it isn't optional.

Friendships are the spiritual habit you're already doing, whether you realize it or not. That's good news, because it means you're already moving somewhere. The challenge now is to steer yourself in the right direction. With a few small steps, you can be on a path to deeper, more meaningful friendships.

Building a friendship habit in the home—for families

- Make It Easy: Don't feel the need to structure all of your kids' play time. Unstructured play with friends provides a ton of benefit—and it's easy on you.

- Make It Tangible: Have your kids make friendship bracelets or hand-drawn cards for their friends.
- Pick a Place: Your local park is designed for kids to have fun—and to connect with each other. When the weather's nice enough, head over and let the magic happen. (You might even make a friend or two yourself . . . if you want.)
- Choose Your Timing: If you already have pizza and movie night on Friday (because you're exhausted), sync up with another family that does the same.
- Make It Playful: Playdates may have been invented for the sanity of parents, but they are also a huge blessing to kids. Make time for your kids to play together with other kids.
- **Find Your Friends: Ask your kids about their friends at school— what they enjoy, what kinds of jokes they like, what they do outside of school. Celebrate friendship like you would any other school achievement.**

Building a friendship habit in the home—for grown-ups

- Make It Easy: Text someone once a week, inviting them to a meal.
- Make It Tangible: Prioritize time in the same place, at the same time over digital connection.
- Pick a Place: When you meet to hang out, make the place a good one—like the firepit or a coffee shop, not the garage.
- Choose Your Timing: When starting a new spiritual habit, start together with someone else.
- Make It Playful: Say yes in advance to most fun invites.
- **Find Your Friends: Do a brief audit of your friends. List as many as you can think of. Then select three or four that you consider your closest friends. Text them to let them know how grateful you are for them. Not only will they appreciate it, but it will draw you even closer together.**

God Finishes

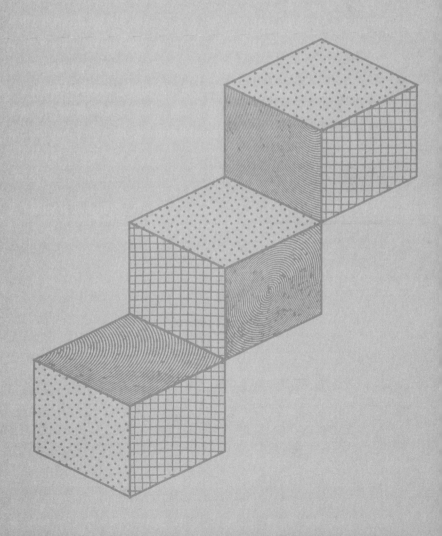

CONCLUSION

- Failure is part of the process.

- The path to new habits is filled with bumps and bruises—and second chances.

- God doesn't just start. God finishes.

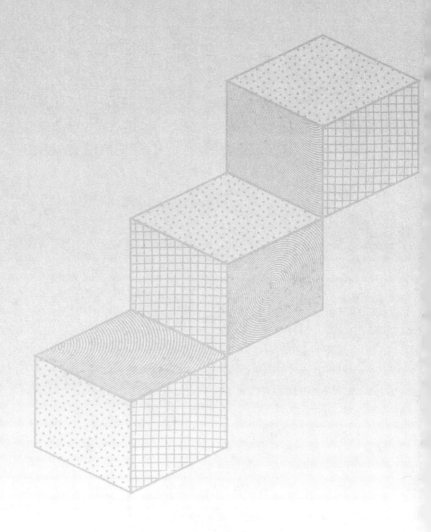

"Congratulations, You Failed!"

n the 2007 animated movie *Meet the Robinsons*, the main character, a bright orphan named Lewis, is trying to work out the kinks of his peanut-butter-and-jelly shooter. The invention has been giving him fits—it even blasted a mess onto a potential adoptive dad who, it turned out, was severely allergic to peanut butter—but Lewis feels like he's close to a breakthrough.

Then, one day, at dinner with a kooky but friendly family (the Robinsons), he has his moment. Uncle Joe wants a PB&J, so Lewis decides to test out the peanut-butter-and-jelly shooter. It clicks, it whirs, and it looks like it's about to work its magic . . . until suddenly, it explodes, covering everyone at the table with splotches of jelly and peanut butter.

Lewis is crushed. He begins to apologize. But before he can say "I'm sorry," the entire table erupts in cheers. "Congratulations!" they all cry. "You failed!" And not in a mocking tone, either. In genuine jubilation. Now Lewis is stunned.

Why all this celebration over failure? As one of the family members puts it, "From failing, you learn. From success? Not so much." This strange family had embraced failure as a necessary step on the road to innovation and creativity. Pretty soon, Lewis does, too.

What is true for animated kid geniuses is true for all of us. We resent failure. We resist failure. We do everything in our power to avoid failure. But when learning new habits, we actually *need* failures to help us grow.

The authors of *Influencer* note that if people *only* experience success in the early stages of the learning process, later failures will be crippling. After all, a short history of easy successes can create a false expectation that growth can happen without much effort. Then if people run into a problem, they become discouraged.[1] Not being used to failure, they quit.

On the other hand, experiencing "intermittent defeats" provides people with enough resilience to practice *overcoming* those hurdles. And the more they overcome smaller hurdles, the more they believe they can overcome larger ones.

Have you failed in your attempts at developing spiritual habits? Is your spiritual life a cycle of starts, stops, pauses, and dead ends? Welcome to the club. What I hope you realize, at this point in the book, is that your stumbling attempts shouldn't make you drop your head in shame. Have you failed? Congratulations. It's all part of the process.

BUMPS AND BRUISES AND SECOND CHANCES

Ed Catmull, in his fantastic book about Pixar's culture, *Creativity, Inc.*, takes this line of reasoning one step further. "Mistakes," Catmull argues, "aren't a necessary evil. They aren't evil at all. They are an inevitable consequence of doing something new."[2]

If you're trying to change your spiritual habits, you're doing something dramatically new. Which means, without exception, you will make a ton of mistakes along the way. You can experience those mistakes, those failures, as an indictment on you and your character. *I should pray more; I'm such a terrible person! I haven't read a Bible story with my son in a week; what does that say about me?* Or you can remember that trying something new means making new mistakes. The path of old habits is flat, smooth, mistake-free . . . and uneventful. But the path to new habits is filled with bumps and bruises.

And second chances.

Because, remember, in every step of our spiritual life, *God is gracious*. That means we get second chances. We get third chances. Shoot, look back at your own life and start tallying up the number of times God has been gracious to you. I'm sure your *ten-thousandth* chance is already in your rearview mirror!

God wants to know you. So when you inevitably stumble in your spiritual habits, He is the first to help dust you off. No scolding. No shaking of the head. Instead, like the gentle Father that He is, He says, "This is new. I get it. Let's rest for a moment, then try it again."

The sixteenth-century reformer Martin Luther once quipped, "To progress is always to begin again."[3] Which is excellent advice for all of us who are stumbling and bumbling along in our spiritual habits.

Has your family missed attending church for the past month? *God is gracious* enough to give you another Sunday this weekend. Begin again.

Did you start memorizing Bible verses with your kids, only to have them resist—and for you to give up? *God is gracious* enough to give you other ways of reading the Bible with them. Try something else. Begin again.

Did you make a commitment to pray for your kids every day, only to lose steam after a week? *God is gracious*, He's still listening, and He cares for your kids more than you do. Begin again.

Did you fall off the pace of your Bible reading plan, somewhere around Leviticus? *God is gracious* enough to have His Word available to you tomorrow. It's no less powerful because you missed a few days. So begin again—maybe this time in one of the Gospels.

Did you begin your spiritual habits in grace, only to find yourself back under a yoke of slavery (Gal. 5:1)? *God is gracious* enough to bring you back to those grace-based beginnings. God still *wants to know you,* and He is leaning forward, even today, waiting for you to say, "Help." Begin again.

GOD DOESN'T JUST START

We began this book with the profound truth that *God starts.* All of the good in our lives begins with Him. All of the initiative in our spiritual habits lies with Him. God starts. We respond.

But God doesn't just start this process. As the apostle Paul wrote to the church in Philippi, "I am sure of this, that he who began a good work in you will bring it to completion at the day of Jesus Christ" (Phil. 1:6). God starts. And God always finishes what He starts.

God has started a work in you. He has started a work in your family. Does that work seem small and weak? It may be—for now. Does it seem fragile, like a tiny seed? It may be—at the moment. But God will finish what He has started. Because of His grace, your seedling of faith can grow into an immovable beech tree.

God is going to change you. I know it. And He'll do it like He's done it millions of times before—slowly, slowly, slowly. Immeasurably slowly. Uncomfortably slowly. Frustratingly slowly. But surely.

As you walk in God's rhythm of slowness and sureness, we pray you will respond to God and pay attention to His presence. That you will remember how much *He wants to be with you.* That you will feel the freedom to move *at His pace* and *in His grace.* Because while change comes slower than you might like, it's more sure than you can imagine.

SMALL STEPS YOU CAN TAKE TODAY

All throughout the book, we've provided a recurring section called "Small Steps You Can Take Today," where we offered a few super practical (and super small) applications, building them out as we introduced each principle. We've combined them all here for easy access, so you can see how the principles work for a handful of spiritual habits.

As a reminder, you don't have to do all of this—in fact, you shouldn't. Pick up one or two of the ideas that seem like they'd work for you. And if those don't end up sticking, come back and try one or two of the others.

1. Sabbath: Sabbath is a habit of enjoying what God has given us.

Building a Sabbath habit in the home—for families

- Make It Easy: Just plan a fun, weekly kickoff meal and call it a Sabbath Meal.
- Make It Tangible: Use a special candle or a special plate for the meal. Or create a Sabbath box to put to-do lists and homework in. But remember, small steps means picking one, not both.
- Pick a Place: Sabbath is celebration. Do this somewhere fun. You can do the meal at the same table, but you can also do it outside, or on the floor, or anywhere that makes it a celebration.
- Choose Your Timing: Decide to start at a meal or at whatever time is a landmark of your week. The end of the school week might feel right. Or the night before you go to worship the next morning.
- Make It Playful: Each night at the meal, plan a fun activity for that evening or the next day. Make sure to keep it easy.

- Find Your Friends: If you commit to this type of meal with another family or two, you'll be more likely to do it. You don't have to actually share the meal together, but sometimes you can.

Building a Sabbath habit in the home—for grown-ups

- Make It Easy: Okay, taking a break from our phone is hard, but it's good for us. Don't go cold turkey, attempting twenty-four straight hours without your phone. Instead, find a key moment in your weekly rhythms that already breaks the cycle of work. Decide to kick-start a break from your phone in under five minutes. Just do something to appreciate the week and celebrate God's gifts to you. Then, make sure to use the word *Sabbath*.
- Make It Tangible: Use a Sabbath box to put your work items in. Locking them away really does help.
- Pick a Place: Remember, Sabbath is celebration. Go to a happy place— we mean literally, physically go there—if you can.
- Choose Your Timing: Decide to start at a meal or at whatever time is a landmark of your week.
- Make It Playful: This should be fun. What would make you light up with delight? Try *that* during this upcoming Sabbath.
- Find Your Friends: Do this with a friend or two, inviting them to join you in marking the Sabbath.

2. Prayer: A conversation God has started with us and we continue in many ways.

Building a prayer habit in the home—for families

- Make It Easy: Pray for one thing—just one thing—at bedtime. Literally make it a one-sentence start.
- Make It Tangible: Use popsicle sticks in a jar to rotate through all the requests your little one wants to pray about. Pick one at night, and put it back in upside down when you are done. Repeat. Keep a few blank

popsicle sticks and a pen close by.

- Pick a Place: Put the jar beside the toothbrush or on a bedside table. Try each and see which works better.
- Choose Your Timing: Nighttime seems like a great time. But find the time with the least number of distractions for your family.
- Make It Playful: Let the kids pray what they want. Sure, there's a time for coaching. But don't do it just yet. Especially if they are having a hard time, just have them tell you what they think and feel and want ... then you pray for them as a model.
- Find Your Friends: Got multiple kids? Each kid gets a jar. Neighbors? Friends? Cousins? Pen pals? More people makes it more likely you'll keep it up.

Building a prayer habit in the home—for grown-ups

- Make It Easy: Decide to kneel for thirty seconds in the morning before your day begins.
- Make It Tangible: A kneeling pad is a great tangible item to use for prayer. You can put it by a bed or by a desk. If the goal is to get into the posture, this cue is excellent and helps you actually do the habit.
- Pick a Place: Quiet is important. A grand location can be cool. But more importantly make sure the place is somewhere you pass often.
- Choose Your Timing: Choose a transition time—before work, before bed, after a meal.
- Make It Playful: Conversation is conversation. If you are in a silly mood or very happy, you don't have to change that when you talk to God. If your kid can say it to you without being disrespectful, then you can say it to God.
- Find Your Friends: Add prayer as part of your regular rhythm with people you already know. You don't even have to make it super long or elaborate—literally fifteen seconds is fine. It may feel awkward, especially at first, but we guarantee your friends will appreciate it.

3. Bible Reading: We know God best by knowing His Word. Read it.

Building a Bible-reading habit in the home—for families

- Make It Easy: The Bible is intimidating, but fortunately, there are a lot of great age-appropriate adaptations. Pick one (like David Helm's *Big Picture Story Bible* or Sally Lloyd-Jones' *Jesus Storybook Bible*) and read one story a night. Bite-sized stories with a beginning and an end? That's easy. And if you have elementary readers, try Kaleidoscope Kids' Bibles.[4]

- Make It Tangible: Again, kids' resources already tend to get this right. But make sure to choose a Bible that is inviting, the kind a kid would want to pick up.

- Pick a Place: Where do you and your kids already gather? Their bedroom at the end of the day? The breakfast table? Choose the place that already slows everyone down and has you together. That's where you should put your Bible.

- Choose Your Timing: If your mornings are crazy as you rush out the door, that's not a great time for devotionals. Aim for bedtime instead. Or if you already have a bedtime routine and don't want to rock it, find some other slow moment.

- Make It Playful: During devotions, go with any conversation that pops into their mind (within reason). Engaging with the Bible doesn't mean every night has to be a theology lesson.

- Find Your Friends: Consider adding a side-by-side journal element for older kids, in which you and your kid take turns jotting down notes from the passage and notes to each other. It's a fun way to keep the *together* element of reading alive.

Building a Bible-reading habit in the home—for grown-ups

- Make It Easy: Decide what you are going to read. Just about any reading plan will work. Just pick one—and make sure the pace starts small. You can always increase it.

- Make It Tangible: You probably already have a Bible you got for free somewhere. It's probably hideous. If you don't already have one, go get a beautiful Bible that you actually want to hold.
- Pick a Place: Put the Bible where you will read it. Make sure you pass it at the right time and that the chair you have it by is good for reading. Your place doesn't have to be magnificent to become holy. But it does need to be intentional. Plus, don't be frustrated if you have to change the place a few times. Trial and error is part of the process.
- Choose Your Timing: Afternoons are terrible times to do anything significant—except maybe take a nap. So don't start your Bible reading then. Look to the bookends of your day—morning and evening—and choose the one that feels like it has the most margin.
- Make It Playful: Give yourself permission to choose a translation that is a little more readable. Or, from time to time, pick up a kids' Bible or some other creative adaptation—like *The Bible Recap*,[5] the BibleProject videos,[6] or *The Book of God* by Walter Wangerin, Jr. It's okay to enjoy what you're reading.
- Find Your Friends: Rather than just choosing a reading plan, choose a reading plan with a buddy. Commit to reading that same plan over the course of a few months. The accountability of that other person will help keep you on track.

4. Examen: Reflection that leads to gratitude.

Building an examen habit in the home—for families

- Make It Easy: Keep it incredibly short and don't force it. Sometimes you'll get a deep reflection; other times you'll hear about what your kid ate for lunch. Both are great.
- Make It Tangible: Get a reminder with a list of questions. If your family has tried "a high and a low" or "a rose and a thorn" at dinner, provide some physical object that reminds you to have this conversation.

- Pick a Place: We recommend the dinner table. It's a great place for conversation, and a natural time to reflect on the day. The bedroom at bedtime can also work. (But don't do both.)
- Choose Your Timing: We think dinnertime is the best option for this one. Conversation is open and free-flowing. Your little ones are in one place with your undivided attention. Give this time a little cue toward reflection and you have yourself a spiritual habit.
- Make It Playful: Let kids be kids as they are defining their highs and lows. Don't feel like you have to coach the interpretation every time. Sometimes they will be grateful that they aren't eating brussels sprouts or that tomorrow isn't a school day. And you know what— who wouldn't be?
- Find Your Friends: In this case, your family are your friends. Of course, if you share meals with other people, include them in the action. Most people are open to sharing about their day.

Building an examen habit in the home—for grown-ups

- Make It Easy: Your examen doesn't have to come out as a sermon or well-written blog post. God isn't judging your public speaking or your writing style here.
- Make It Tangible: Get a paper journal, and a nice one. We use a "five-year journal" so we can track our reflections year over year. But you don't have to go so big. Just keep the entries short—literally a sentence or two—so it doesn't feel daunting.
- Pick a Place: Comfy is the name of the game here. A comfy chair should work. Or even your bed. (It's even okay if you fall asleep while you're doing this. Grace!)
- Choose Your Timing: Though we do know people who practice examen first thing in the morning, reflecting on the previous day, the most natural timing seems to be at the very end of the day. But feel free to get creative on the timing. And know that reflection can happen

daily, weekly, monthly, and yearly. Carve out time to review what has happened over that time period. Celebrate God's faithfulness and presence every time you go to bed, flip a calendar, or have a vacation.

- Make It Playful: Let an examen journal be different from your counseling journal. These are *small* memories you're trying to capture, not pages of emotional reflections.
- Find Your Friends: Doing this with your spouse or a trusted friend is great, provided it's a little less frequent. An annual year-in-review with your spouse can be an examen practice. A monthly conversation with a friend can be an examen practice, too—and much less intimidating than "accountability partners."

5. Worship: Sing the truth about God.

Building a worship habit in the home—for families

- Make It Easy: Thankfully, children's worship songs are already pretty easy. Chances are your kids learned the songs before you did. So the toughest part will be *you* learning them! (But trust us: It won't be that tough.) Maybe even pick a playlist or an artist in advance.
- Make It Tangible: Children's worship songs often have hand motions that go along with them. Learn the motions and dance along. Get a Bluetooth speaker you don't mind leaving out in the room.
- Pick a Place: If you've got speakers, put them in the main area of your house. If you've got musical instruments (next level, look at you!), put *those* in the main area of your house. Make music part of the environment.
- Choose Your Timing: When your kids ask, say yes! Songs are the perfect length for a short break, so you can totally commit and still be finished in less than five minutes.
- Make It Playful: Follow your kids' lead here. They may want you to sing in a silly voice. Go for it. They may want to use that obnoxious

microphone their aunt got them last Christmas. Give it a whirl.

- Find Your Friends: Singing alone is good. But studies show that singing together multiplies the benefits.[7] So sing along with your kids!

Building a worship habit in the home—for grown-ups

- Make It Easy: Our churches have already made this one as simple as possible. Every single church we know uses music as part of the service. So go . . . and sing!
- Make It Tangible: If you can read music, get a copy of a hymnal. If you can play, make your instrument easily accessible. And if you can't do any of that, this is a moment where your phone may actually help you out—"favorite" a few worship songs so your music-streaming app starts sprinkling those into your regular mix.
- Pick a Place: Music can become an essential part of the environment for many of your spiritual habits. Consider using worship music along with your other spiritual rhythms (like prayer or Bible reading).
- Choose Your Timing: You probably already listen to music—in the car, at the gym. Rotate some worship music into the music you already listen to.
- Make It Playful: Do you ever have a song stuck in your head? Throughout the day, you'll hum it to yourself. Well, rather than muttering it under your breath, really go for it. Sing out loud!
- Find Your Friends: Share your favorite worship songs with your friends and ask for their favorites, too.

6. Friends: Community can be messy and confusing and beautiful and fun—but it isn't optional.

Building a friendship habit in the home—for families

- Make It Easy: Don't feel the need to structure all of your kids' play time. Unstructured play with friends provides a ton of benefit—and it's easy on you.

- Make It Tangible: Have your kids make friendship bracelets or hand-drawn cards for their friends.
- Pick a Place: Your local park is designed for kids to have fun—and to connect with each other. When the weather's nice enough, head over and let the magic happen. (You might even make a friend or two yourself . . . if you want.)
- Choose Your Timing: If you already have pizza and movie night on Friday (because you're exhausted), sync up with another family that does the same.
- Make It Playful: Playdates may have been invented for the sanity of parents, but they are also a huge blessing to kids. Make time for your kids to play together with other kids.
- Find Your Friends: Ask your kids about their friends at school—what they enjoy, what kinds of jokes they like, what they do outside of school. Celebrate friendship like you would any other school achievement.

Building a friendship habit in the home—for grown-ups

- Make It Easy: Text someone once a week, inviting them to a meal.
- Make It Tangible: Prioritize time in the same place, at the same time over digital connection.
- Pick a Place: When you meet to hang out, make the place a good one—like the firepit or a coffee shop, not the garage.
- Choose Your Timing: When starting a new spiritual habit, start together with someone else.
- Make It Playful: Say yes in advance to most fun invites.
- Find Your Friends: Do a brief audit of your friends. List as many as you can think of. Then select three or four that you consider your closest friends. Text them to let them know how grateful you are for them. Not only will they appreciate it, but it will draw you even closer together.

I will

_____

(MAKE IT EASY)

when _____

(CHOOSE YOUR TIMING)

in _____

(PICK A PLACE)

and use _____

(MAKE IT TANGIBLE)

to cue me to start.

I will do this with

_____

(FIND YOUR FRIENDS)

and _____

(MAKE IT PLAYFUL)

to keep it engaging for my whole family.

▢ MAKE IT EASY

- Forgive yourself.
- Make it easier than you think.
- Write it down.

▢ MAKE IT TANGIBLE

- Set a cue that...
  - ... you can touch.
  - ... you trip over.
  - ... distracts you from your phone.
  - ... works for you, not for us.

▢ PICK A PLACE

- A convenient place you pass often.
- A place that is inviting and free of distractions.
- A place that has items conducive to the spiritual habit.

▢ CHOOSE YOUR TIMING

- Day to day, prioritize evening and morning
- Season to season, pay attention to temporal landmarks.
- Embrace the grace of the restart.

▢ MAKE IT PLAYFUL

- Be playful!
- Play is a spiritual habit.
- Say yes in advance to the playful moment.

▢ FIND YOUR FRIENDS

- Friends increase our confidence.
- Friends give us encouragement.
- Friends provide accountability.
- Friends multiply our enjoyment.
- Friends fix our mistakes.
- Friends give us a sense of purpose.

ACKNOWLEDGMENTS

f you're reading this, one of two things is true of you: (1) You read the Acknowledgments section of every book, because does it count if you skip it? Or (2) You're looking for your name.

If you're in Group 1, you officially have our permission to skip this section. Well, in *other* books. You should totally keep reading this one.

If you're in Group 2, we sure hope you find your name below. (But don't panic: We left *one name* out on purpose. In fact, it's the most important person of all—so that's probably you.)

First and foremost, thanks to our inquisitive kids—Cara and Susan Greene; and Lottie and Teddy Pappalardo. Your brilliant and challenging questions push us to understand our faith in a way we never had before. ("Did Jonah really live in a whale's belly for three days?") We hope and pray that you have full lives of faith, walking with God and your neighbors.

Thanks to Jenn Pappalardo and Kristen Greene. We live all of this out with you. Thank you for your honest and real feedback every time we say, "Hey, what do you think about . . . ?" Our spiritual life is richer because of you.

A heaping helping of thanks to the other members of our GoodKind team: Brian Turney, Lindsey Love, and Amy Kavanaugh. You'll recognize our team's core values all throughout this book. After all, we've all been figuring out these "small steps" together for the last four years. Growing this small business hasn't always been easy, but it's always been a blessing.

Thanks to the crew at Sherpa Collaborative: Arthur Tew, Pete Pagano, and Mark Saad. Without you, GoodKind wouldn't exist—and neither would this book.

Thanks to our agent, Don Gates, who helped us see what this book could be even before we could.

Thanks to all of the people who offered helpful feedback on early (sometimes *very* early) drafts of the book: Matt Love, Danny Franks, Eric Stortz, Janetta Oni, Amy Kavanaugh, and Clayton's Third Camp friends. Without your insights, this book would not only have been more confusing; it also would have been much, much longer.

A special shoutout to our youngest test reader, Lottie Pappalardo, who, even in fourth grade, quickly spotted several of our copy errors. (Moody, maybe save a spot for her in a few years?)

Speaking of Moody, every author claims to have the best editorial team out there. But statistically, one of them has to be telling the truth, right? We want to make the case that we've got it. Catherine Parks, our editor, understood what we were trying to do right away. She encouraged us when we were on the right track and redirected us when we were losing our way. As an added bonus, she is simply one of the most delightful people we've ever met.

The rest of the crew at Moody Publishers deserve a big round of thanks, too. Phil Newman, our developmental editor, gave this draft the final polish it needed. Brittany Schrock, the designer, translated the tone of this book beautifully from text to imagery, a task that still feels like alchemy to us. And Avrie Roberts, the copy editor, saved us from sounding downright foolish. If any of you make your way to the Triangle, we will buy you dinner.

Thanks to everyone who has ever purchased Advent Blocks. As we solve problems of spiritual habits for our families, we are always thinking about you. We want to share with you as much as is helpful and not a bit more. Thank you for joining us on this grace-filled journey of starts and stops . . . and restarts.

Finally, thanks to you, our reader. We know your time is precious, so we appreciate you spending it with us. We're praying it bears fruit in your life—not just in the days ahead, but for decades to come.

NOTES

INTRODUCTION: THE HUNT FOR CONGRUENCE

1. Eugene H. Peterson, *As Kingfishers Catch Fire: A Conversation on the Ways of God Formed by the Words of God* (Colorado Springs: WaterBrook, 2017), xvii–xix. Peterson's use of the term "congruence" almost certainly draws from the field of social psychology, where the term has been used for years. Psychologist Carl Rogers described "congruence" as the state in which a person's self-image matches their "ideal self." Another way to put it: A congruent person's *heart* matches their *head*. Saul Mcleod, "Carl Rogers Humanistic Theory and Contribution to Psychology," Simply Psychology, January 29, 2024; https://www.simplypsychology.org/carl-rogers.html.

2. See James Clear, *Atomic Habits: An Easy & Proven Way to Build Good Habits & Break Bad Ones* (New York: Random House, 2018).

CHAPTER 1: WHO GOD IS (AND WHAT THAT MEANS FOR YOUR SPIRITUAL HABITS)

1. Philip Yancey, *What's So Amazing About Grace?* (Grand Rapids, MI: Zondervan, 1997), 45.

CHAPTER 2: WHAT IS A SPIRITUAL HABIT, ANYWAY?

1. James K. A. Smith, *How to Inhabit Time: Understanding the Past, Facing the Future, Living Faithfully Now* (Grand Rapids, MI: Brazos Press, 2022), 128–29.

2. Andy Crouch, *The Tech-Wise Family: Everyday Steps for Putting Technology in Its Proper Place* (Grand Rapids, MI: Baker Books, 2017), 191.

CHAPTER 3: MAKE IT EASY

1. I know this is a fictional anecdote, but I feel the need to be crystal clear here: Kristen is dead wrong with this statement, because Nicolas Cage is a gem.

(Some might even call him a national treasure.) I don't want anyone walking away from this book with the wrong impression.

2. The term "decision fatigue" was coined in 2011 by social psychologist Roy F. Baumeister. John Tierney, "Do You Suffer from Decision Fatigue?," *New York Times*, August 17, 2011, https://www.nytimes.com/2011/08/21/magazine/do-you-suffer-from-decision-fatigue.html.

3. Chip Heath and Dan Heath, *Switch: How to Change Things When Change Is Hard* (New York: Crown Currency, 2010), 52.

4. James Clear, *Atomic Habits: An Easy & Proven Way to Build Good Habits & Break Bad Ones* (New York: Random House, 2018), 71.

5. Heath, *Switch*, 17.

6. Clear, *Atomic Habits*, 153.

7. Ibid., 162.

8. *Mary Poppins*, directed by Robert Stevenson (Burbank, CA: Walt Disney Productions, 1964).

CHAPTER 4: MAKE IT TANGIBLE

1. There are several versions of this out there. Here's the one I saw (and yes, it really did trick me): https://youtu.be/xNSgmm9FX2s?si=g60hXIhtttODU8LX.

2. John Mark Comer, *The Ruthless Elimination of Hurry: How to Stay Emotionally Healthy and Spiritually Alive in the Chaos of the Modern World* (Colorado Springs: WaterBrook, 2019), 54.

3. Ibid., 219–44.

4. Personal conversation with Matthew Sleeth. Dr. Sleeth's book on Sabbath, *24/6: A Prescription for a Healthier, Happier Life* (Carol Stream, IL: Tyndale House, 2012), is well worth the read.

5. Thanks to Amy Kavanaugh for pointing us to this passage to illustrate this idea!

6. Kerry Patterson et al., *Influencer: The New Science of Leading Change* (New York: McGraw Hill Education, 2013), 83.

7. James Clear, *Atomic Habits: An Easy & Proven Way to Build Good Habits & Break Bad Ones* (New York: Random House, 2018), 86.

8. Andy Crouch, *The Tech-Wise Family: Everyday Steps for Putting Technology in Its Proper Place* (Grand Rapids, MI: Baker Books, 2017), 35.

9. My favorite is still Andy Crouch's *Tech-Wise Family*, which is both insightful and beautifully written. Sociologist Sherry Turkle's *Reclaiming Conversation: The Power of Talk in a Digital Age* is another great one, especially when it comes to the issue of technology and attention. For a more accessible and

playful approach, John Mark Comer's *The Ruthless Elimination of Hurry* is a delight. And Justin Whitmel Earley has written helpfully about cultivating wise tech habits in his books *The Common Rule: Habits of Purpose for an Age of Distraction* and *Habits of the Household: Practicing the Story of God in Everyday Family Rhythms*. I tend to geek out about this stuff. So don't feel the need to read all these. But great stuff is out there if you're interested.

CHAPTER 5: PICK A PLACE

1. If you want to explore it yourself, this bookstore-toilet connection is often called the "Mariko Aoki phenomenon." Legitimate research (in English, anyway) is a bit tough to find, but here's a decent summary of the phenomenon: Jonathan Jarry, "The Unbearable Poopness of Bookstores," January 22, 2022, McGill University, https://www.mcgill.ca/oss/article/general-science/unbearable-poopness-bookstores.
2. James Clear, *Atomic Habits: An Easy & Proven Way to Build Good Habits & Break Bad Ones* (New York: Random House, 2018), 84.
3. "How Much is 1 Ton of Gold Worth?," BullionByPost (Birmingham, UK), https://www.bullionbypost.com/index/gold/how-much-is-one-ton-of-gold-worth/.
4. Boyce Rensberger, "Solomon's Mine Believed Found," *New York Times*, May 24, 1976, https://www.nytimes.com/1976/05/24/archives/solomons-mine-believed-found-75249297.html.
5. Lily Bernheimer, *The Shaping of Us: How Everyday Spaces Structure Our Lives, Behaviour, and Well-Being* (San Antonio, TX: Trinity University Press, 2017), 146.
6. Kaleidoscope–Kids' Bibles Reimagined, https://readkaleidoscope.com.

CHAPTER 6: CHOOSE YOUR TIMING

1. James K. A. Smith, *How to Inhabit Time: Understanding the Past, Facing the Future, Living Faithfully Now* (Grand Rapids, MI: Brazos Press, 2022), 102.
2. Daniel Pink, *When: The Scientific Secrets of Perfect Timing* (New York: Riverhead Books, 2018), 54–60.
3. Ibid., 32.
4. Ibid., 26–40.
5. Eugene H. Peterson, *Working the Angles: The Shape of Pastoral Integrity* (Grand Rapids, MI: Eerdmans, 1987), 68.

6. James Clear, *Atomic Habits: An Easy & Proven Way to Build Good Habits & Break Bad Ones* (New York: Random House, 2018), 79.

7. Pink, *When*, 93.

8. Smith, *How to Inhabit Time*, 61.

CHAPTER 7: MAKE IT PLAYFUL

1. Catherine Price, *The Power of Fun: How to Feel Alive Again* (New York: Random House, 2023), 17.

2. Mike Rucker, *The Fun Habit: How the Pursuit of Joy and Wonder Can Change Your Life* (New York: Simon & Schuster, 2023), 5.

3. Price, *The Power of Fun*, 76.

4. G. K. Chesterton, *Orthodoxy* (Colorado Springs: Shaw Books, 2001), 20.

5. Stuart Brown with Christopher Vaughan, *Play: How It Shapes the Brain, Opens the Imagination, and Invigorates the Soul* (New York: Penguin, 2009), 5.

6. Ibid.

7. Ibid.

8. Ibid., 6.

9. Ibid., 17.

10. Price, *The Power of Fun*, 18.

11. Ibid.

12. Brown and Vaughan, *Play*, 7.

13. Brené Brown, *The Gifts of Imperfection: Let Go of Who You Think You're Supposed to Be and Embrace Who You Are* (Center City, MN: Hazelden Publishing, 2010), 128.

14. Brown, *The Gifts of Imperfection*, 127.

15. Price, *The Power of Fun*, 37.

16. Ibid., 34.

CHAPTER 8: FIND YOUR FRIENDS

1. We've often seen this pithy statement summarized as "an African proverb." The sentiment certainly matches many of the more communally minded societies of sub-Saharan Africa. But there isn't any clear source for the quote. Best we can tell, the current phrasing was influenced by an African proverb but popularized by an American author, Bill Hull, in his book *Choose the Life: Exploring a Faith That Embraces Discipleship* (Grand Rapids, MI: Baker Books, 2004), 107. See also Andrew Whitby, "Who First Said: If You Want

to Go Fast, Go Alone; If You Want to Go Far, Go Together?," blog, https://andrewwhitby.com/2020/12/25/if-you-want-to-go-fast/.

2. Daniel H. Pink, *When: The Scientific Secrets of Perfect Timing* (New York: Riverhead Books, 2018), 103, 181; Kerry Patterson et al., *Influencer: The New Science of Leading Change* (New York: McGraw Hill Education, 2013), 203, 208; Mike Rucker, *The Fun Habit: How the Pursuit of Joy and Wonder Can Change Your Life* (New York: Simon & Schuster, 2023), 127.

3. Charles Duhigg, *Power of Habit: Why We Do What We Do in Life and Business* (New York: Random House, 2012), 85.

4. Pink, *When*, 181.

5. Pink, *When*, 103; Patterson et al., *Influencer*, 203, 208.

6. Pink, *When*, 181; Patterson et al., *Influencer*, 210.

7. Justin Whitmel Earley, *Made for People: Why We Drift into Loneliness and How to Fight for a Life of Friendship* (Grand Rapids, MI: Zondervan, 2023), 200.

8. The word for "man" in Hebrew is *adam*, so Genesis 2:18 could be read either as "It is not good that the man is alone" or "It is not good that Adam is alone" (as I've put it here).

9. As a starter, we'd suggest Michael Reeves's book *Delighting in the Trinity: An Introduction to the Christian Faith* (Westmont, IL: IVP Academic, 2012).

10. Rucker, *The Fun Habit*, 120.

11. Chip Heath and Dan Heath, *The Power of Moments: Why Certain Experiences Have Extraordinary Impact* (New York: Simon & Schuster, 2017), 211.

CONCLUSION: GOD FINISHES

1. Kerry Patterson et al., *Influencer: The New Science of Leading Change* (New York: McGraw Hill Education, 2013), 133.

2. Ed Catmull and Amy Wallace, *Creativity, Inc.: Overcoming the Unseen Forces That Stand in the Way of True Inspiration* (New York: Random House, 2014), 7.

3. "*Stare in via Dei, hoc est retrocedere, et proficere, hoc est semper de novo incipere.*" Pauck's translation reads, "To go forward means ever to begin anew." Martin Luther, *Lectures on Romans*, The Library of Christian Classics, vol. 15, trans. and ed. Wilhelm Pauck (Philadelphia: Westminster Press, 1961), 370.

4. Kaleidoscope–Kids' Bibles Reimagined, https://readkaleidoscope.com.

5. Tara-Leigh Cobble, *The Bible Recap: A One-Year Guide to Reading and Understanding the Entire Bible* (Bloomington, MN: Bethany House, 2020). Learn more at: https://www.thebiblerecap.com/.

6. BibleProject, https://bibleproject.com/explore/.

7. Alexandra Moe, "Singing Is Good for You. Singing with Others May Be Even Better," *Washington Post*, June 25, 2023, https://www.washingtonpost.com/wellness/2023/06/25/singing-with-others-mental-physical-health/.

ABOUT THE AUTHORS

Chris Pappalardo, PhD, is a pastor, editor, and writer at The Summit Church in the Raleigh-Durham, North Carolina, area. He is married to Jenn and is the proud dad of Lottie (who wants to save the planet) and Teddy (who wants you to read him another book).

Clayton Greene is the Summit Collaborative Director, where he supports more than seventy (and growing!) independent church plants. He and his wife, Kristen, live in Durham, North Carolina, with their two daughters, Cara and Susan.

Together, Chris and Clayton founded GoodKind, an organization that helps people cultivate the *good kind* of habits and holiday celebrations. Good-Kind began in 2020 when Chris and Clayton created Advent Blocks, a devotional practice that helps kids—and parents—anticipate Jesus all throughout December. Chris, Clayton, and the GoodKind team have been creating beautiful, tangible, and easy discipleship products ever since.

To learn more about GoodKind, go to goodkind.shop.

Here's a small step you can take today!

Founded by authors Chris and Clayton, GoodKind exists to help people engage with God and one another throughout the year with tangible, meaningful products.

Check out what GoodKind has to offer at
www.goodkind.shop

ADVENT BLOCKS

A meaningful family practice to help you anticipate Jesus at Christmas.

GRATIKUBE

Add gratitude, intentionality, and variety into your everyday table conversations.

STICKY PRAYERS

Tangible and beautiful nudges toward a growing habit of prayer.

EASTER BLOCKS

Slow down and savor Christ during Holy Week.

goodkind

You finished reading!

Did this book help you in some way? If so, please consider writing an honest review wherever you purchase your books. Your review gets this book into the hands of more readers and helps us continue to create biblically faithful resources.

Moody Publishers books help fund the training of students for ministry around the world.

The **Moody Bible Institute** is one of the most well-known Christian institutions in the world, training thousands of young people to faithfully serve Christ wherever He calls them. And when you buy and read a book from Moody Publishers, you're helping make that vital ministry training possible.

Continue to dive into the Word, *anytime, anywhere.*

Find what you need to take your next step in your walk with Christ: from uplifting music to sound preaching, our programs are designed to help you right when you need it.

Download the **Moody Radio App** and start listening today!

MOODY
Publishers

MOODY
Bible Institute

MOODY
Radio